COLORING BOOKS
FOR SENIORS
HEART DESIGNS

▲ ART THERAPY COLORING

Preview of Coloring Pages

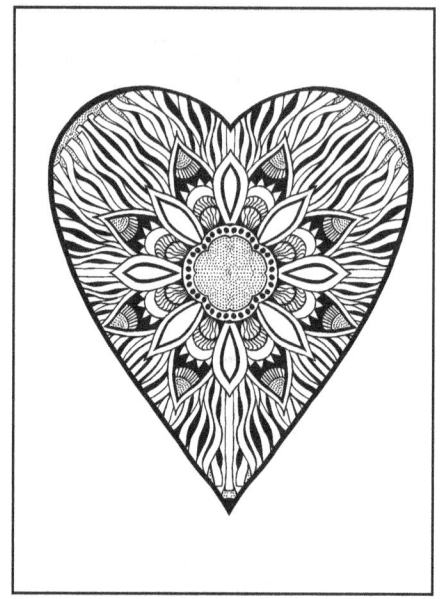
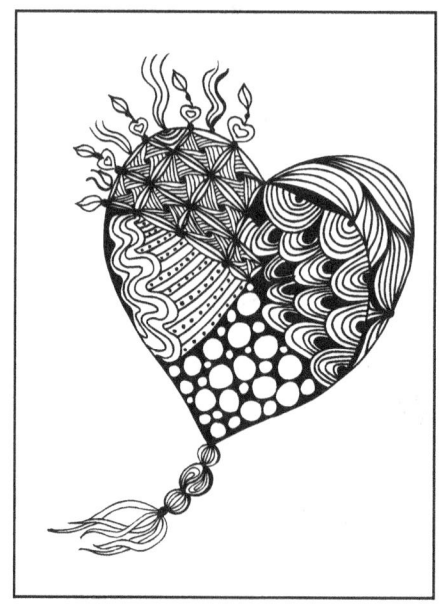
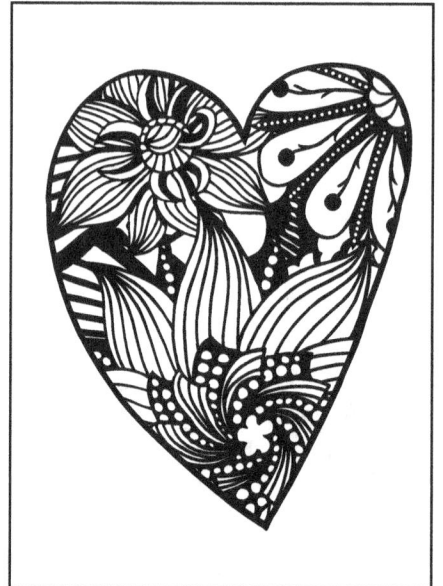
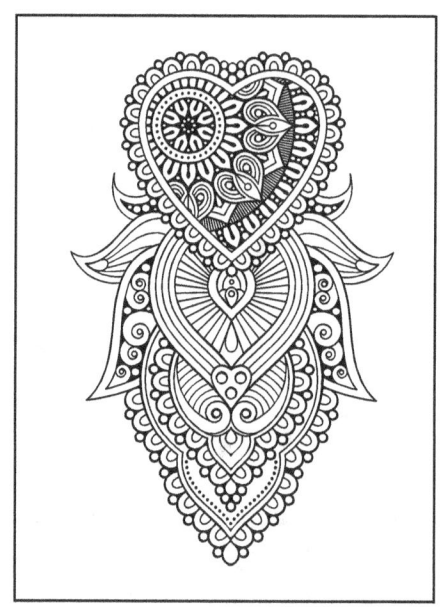
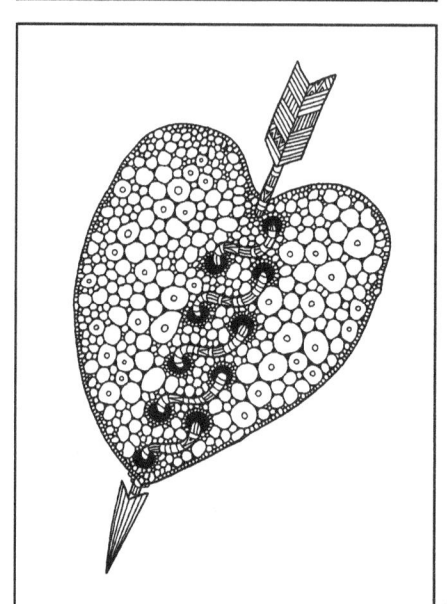
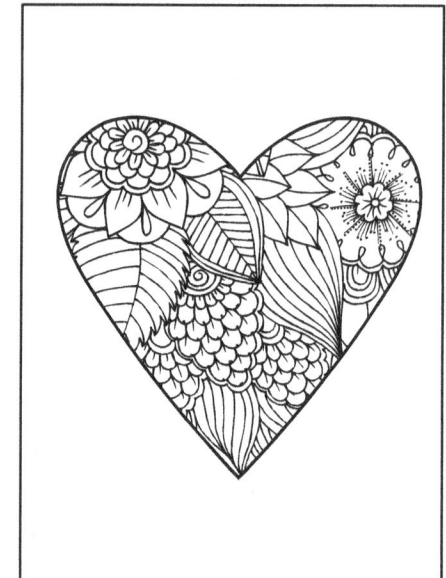
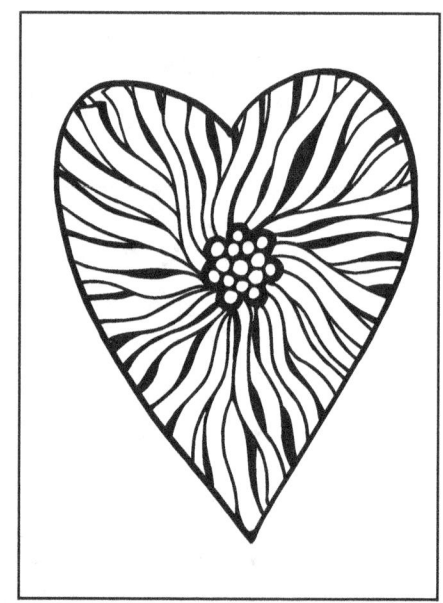
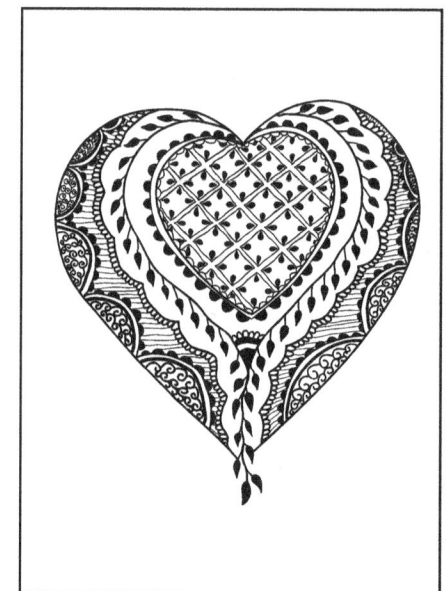
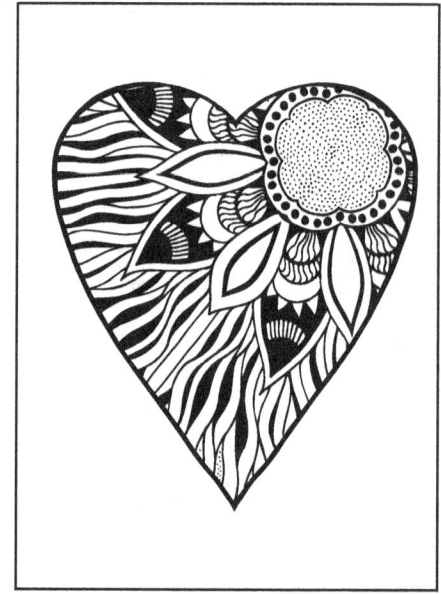

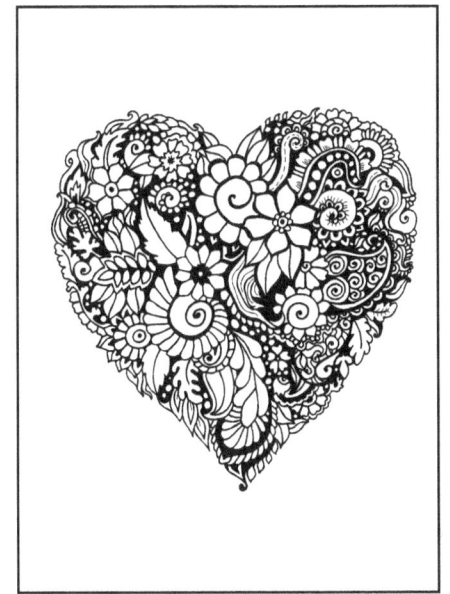
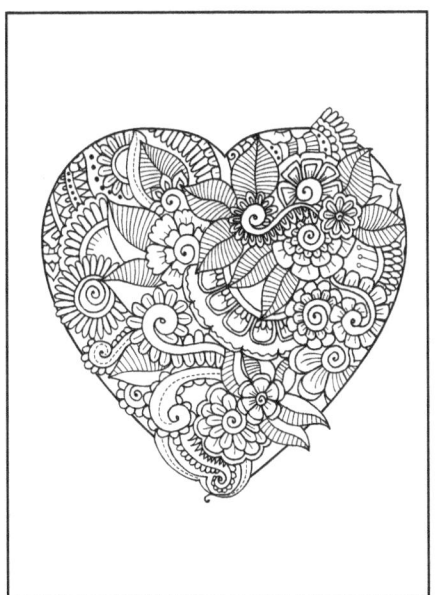
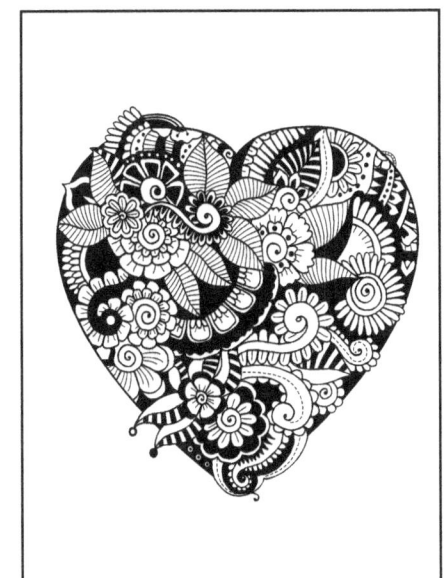

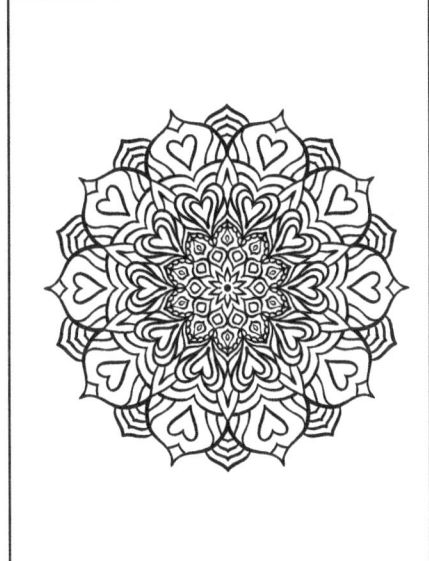
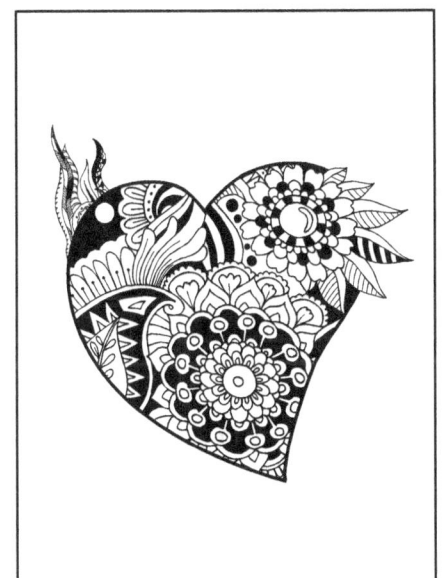

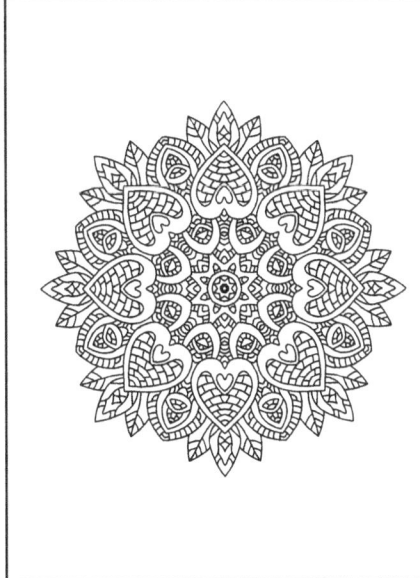
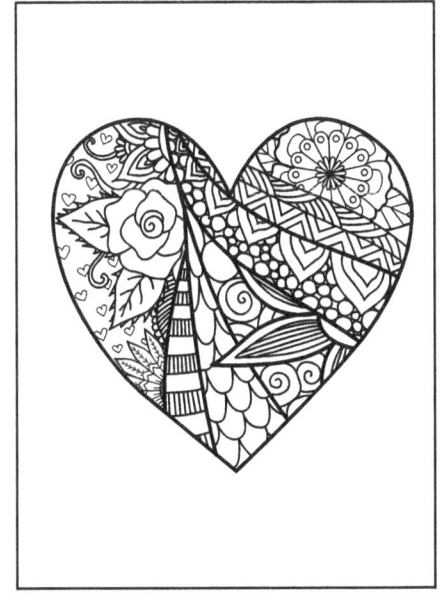

Preview of Coloring Pages

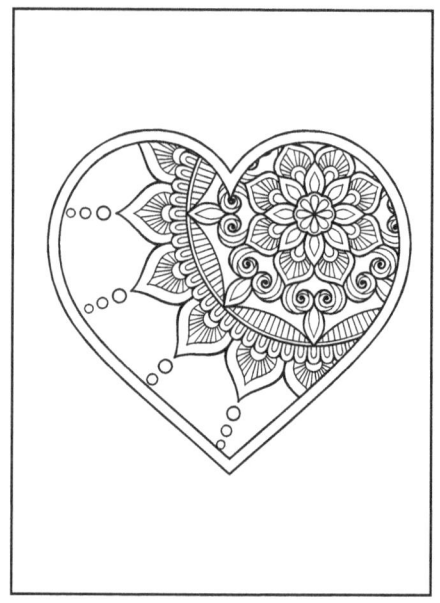
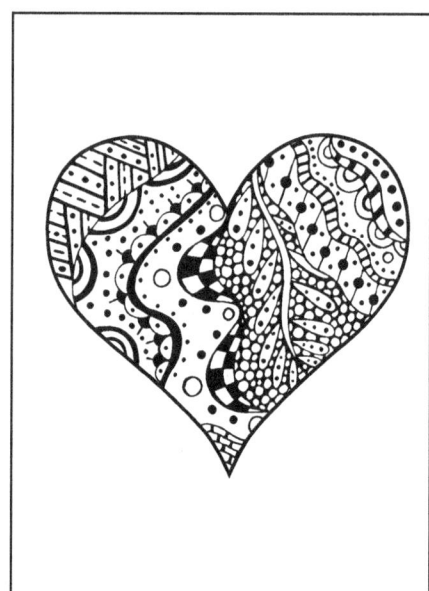
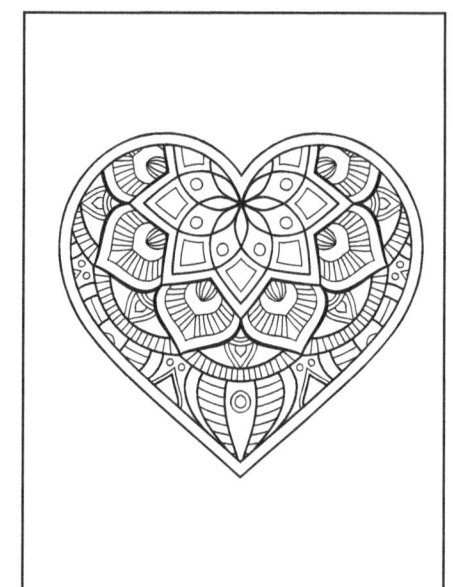
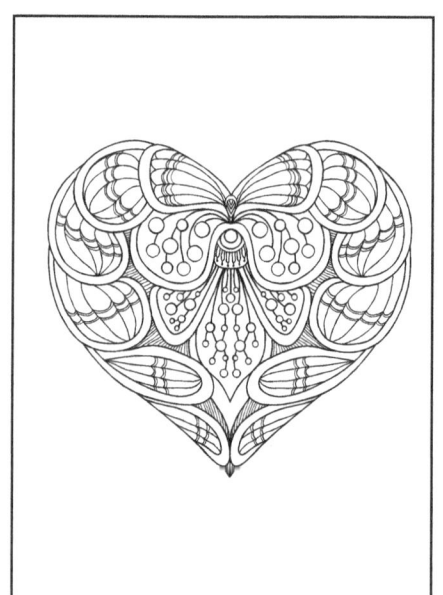
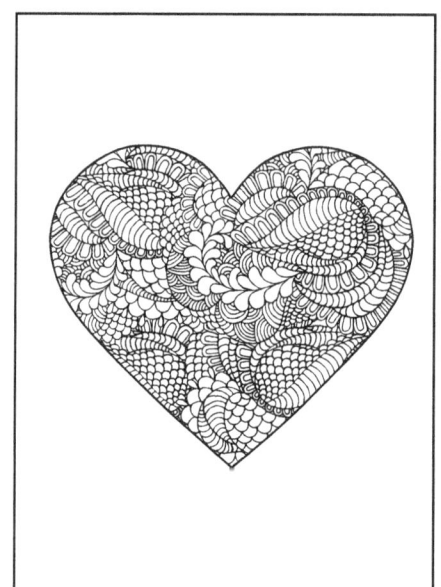
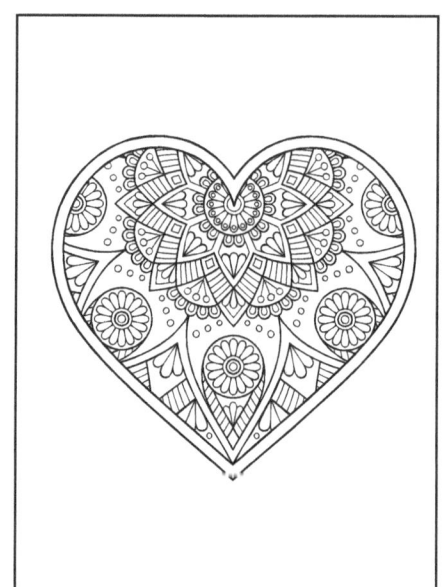

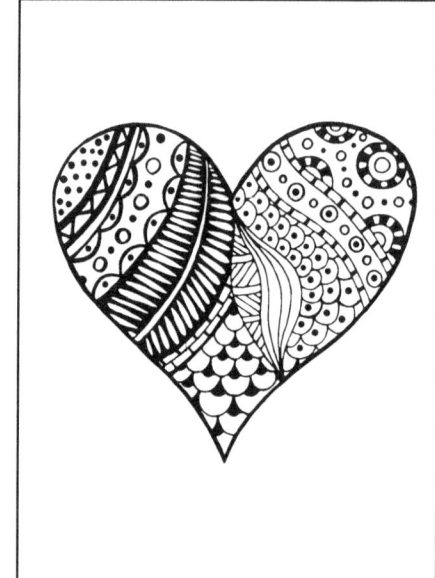
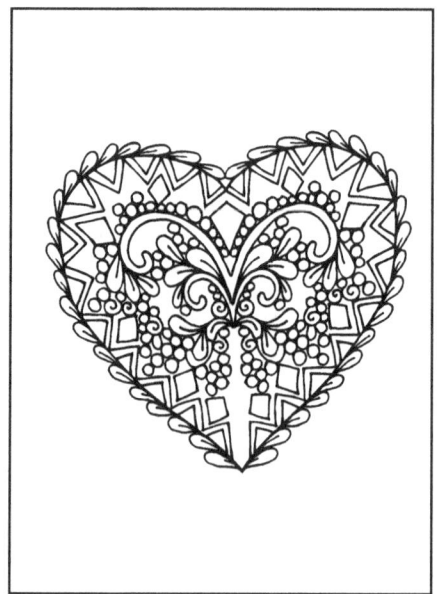

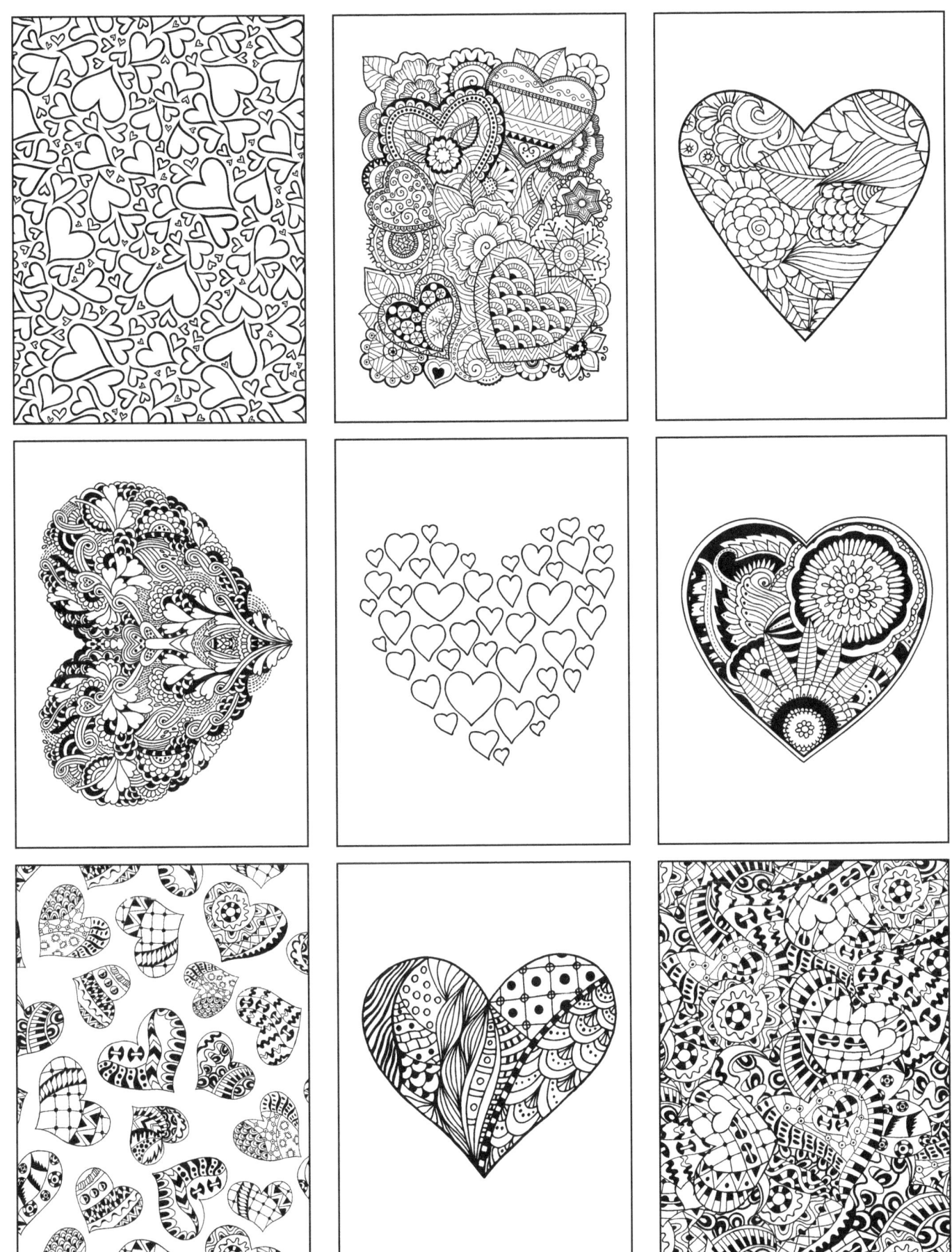

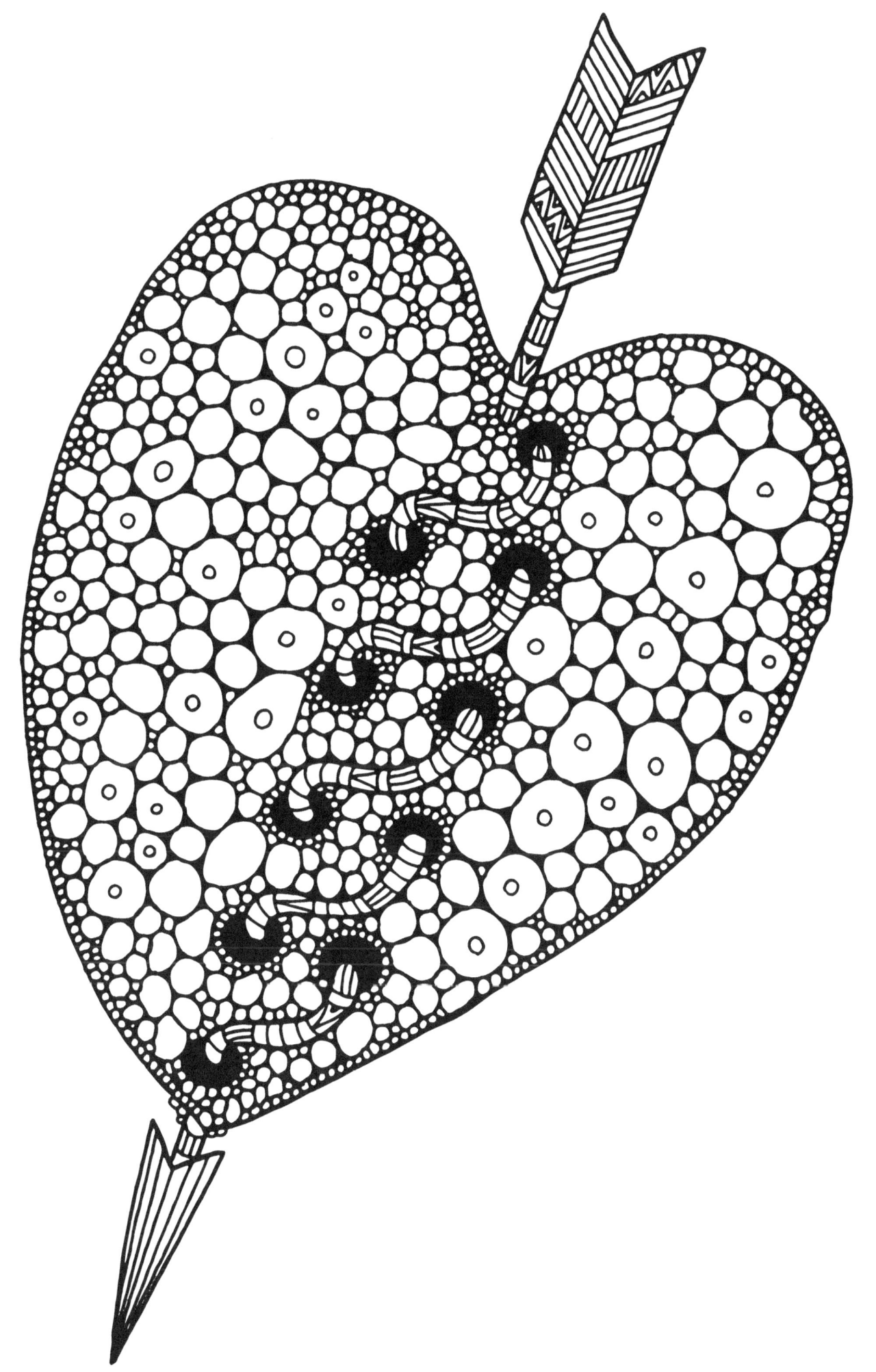

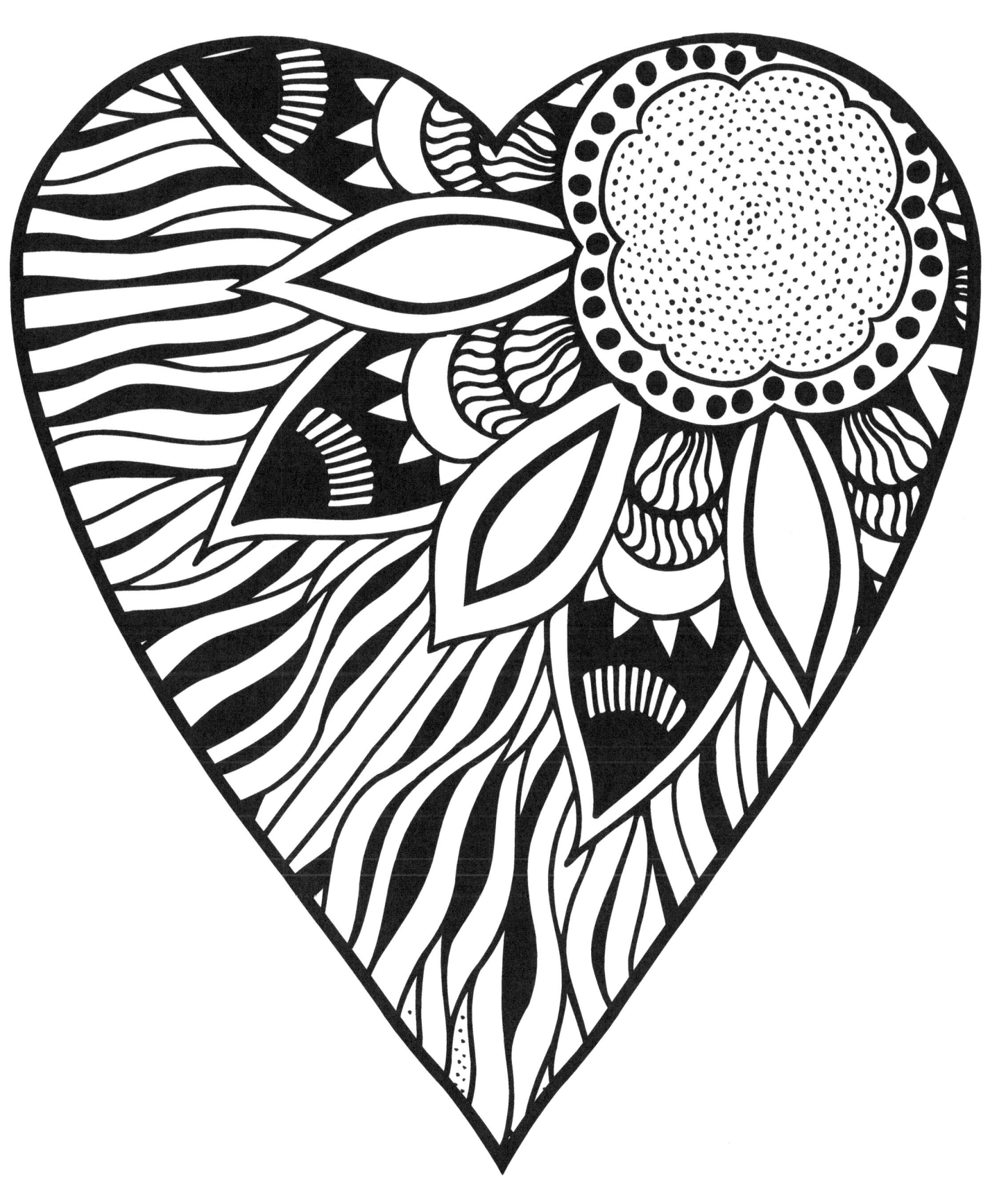

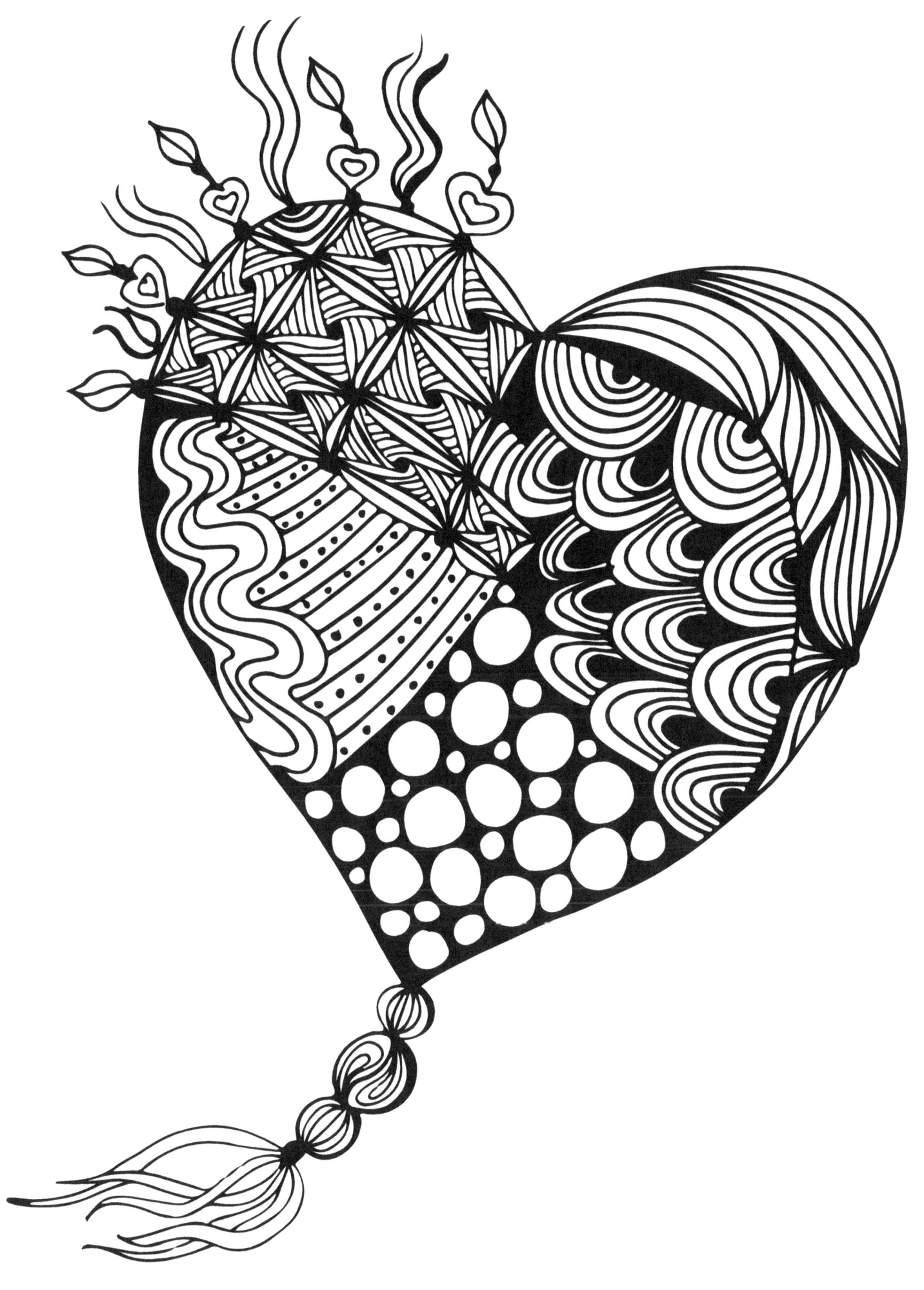

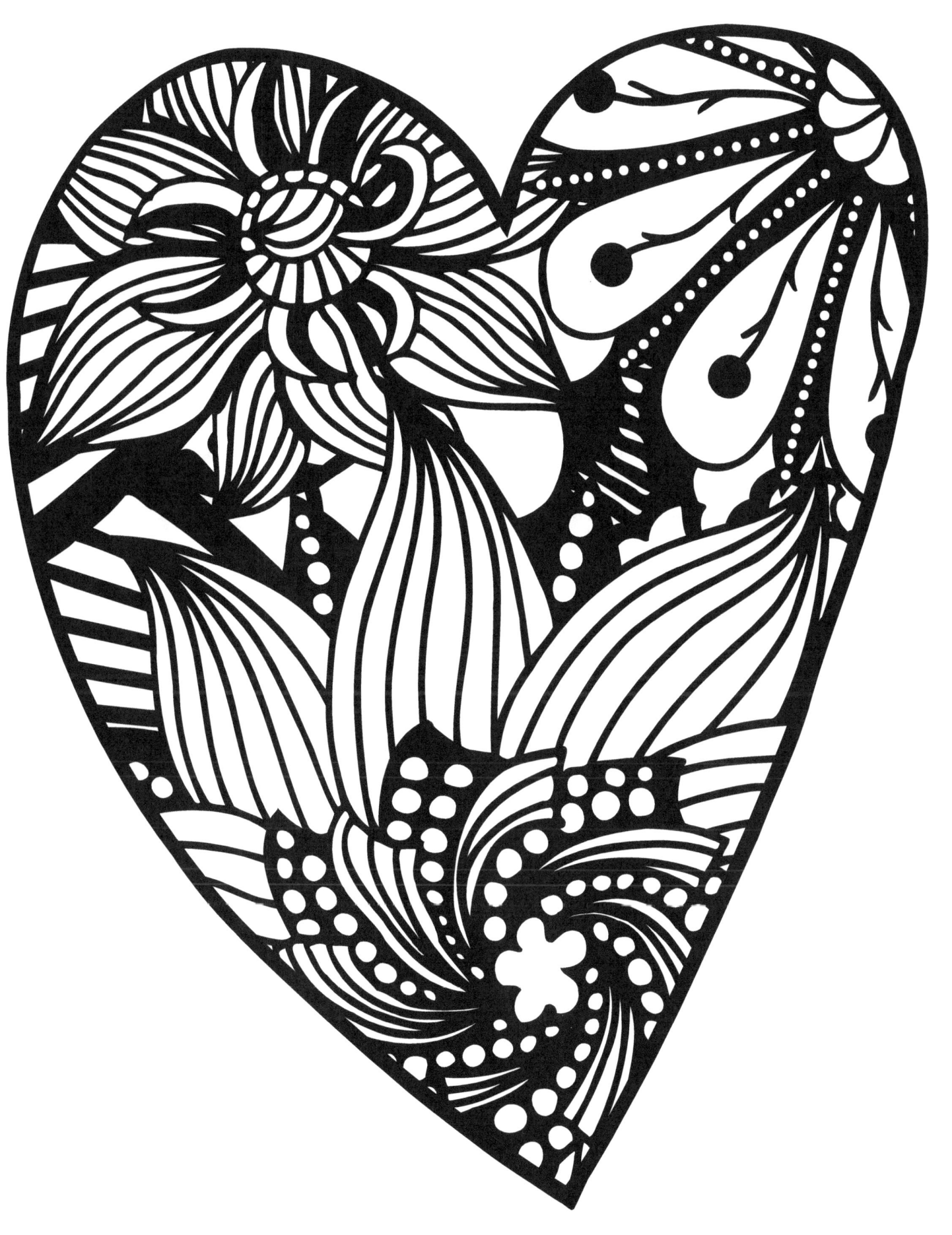

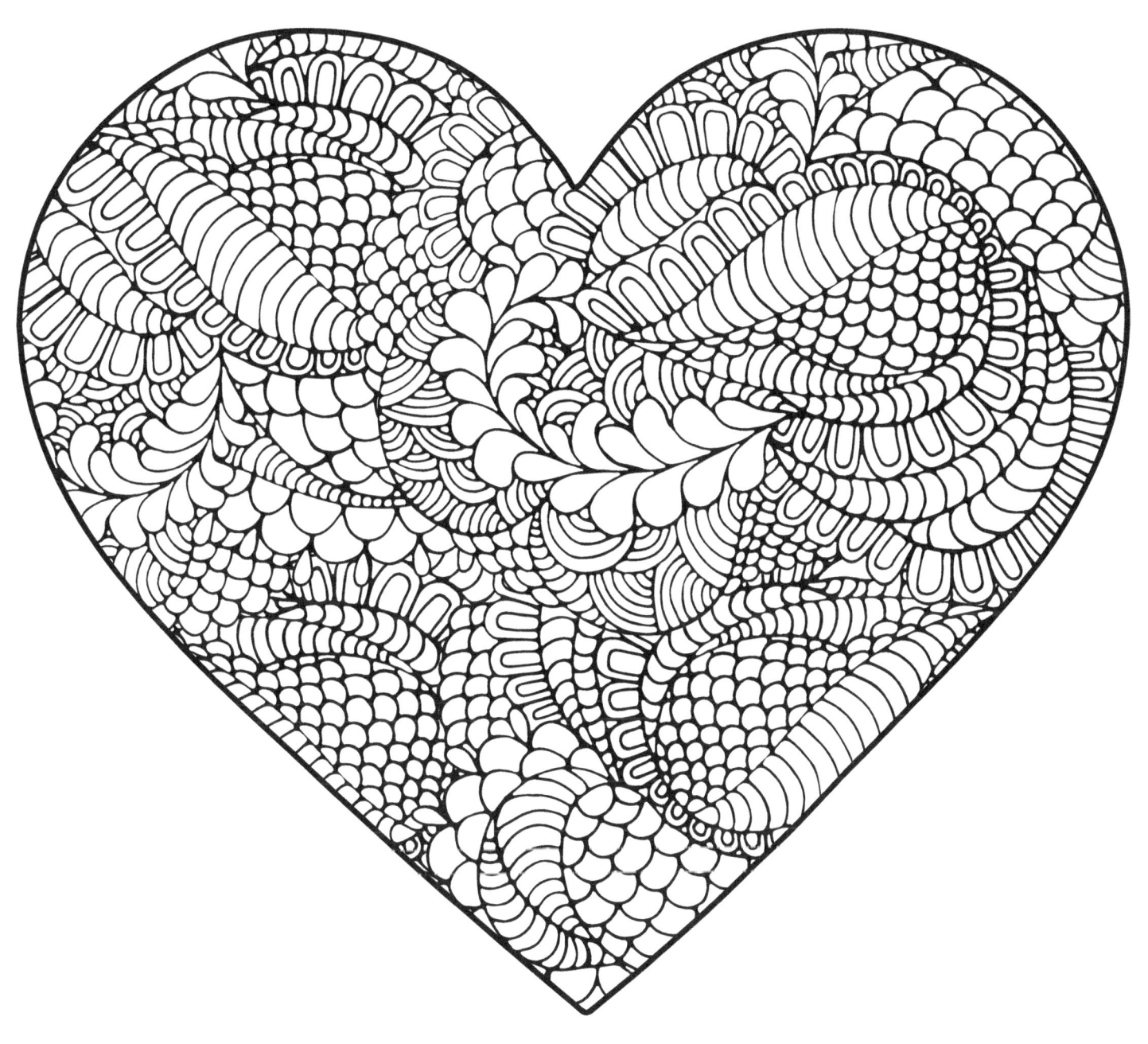

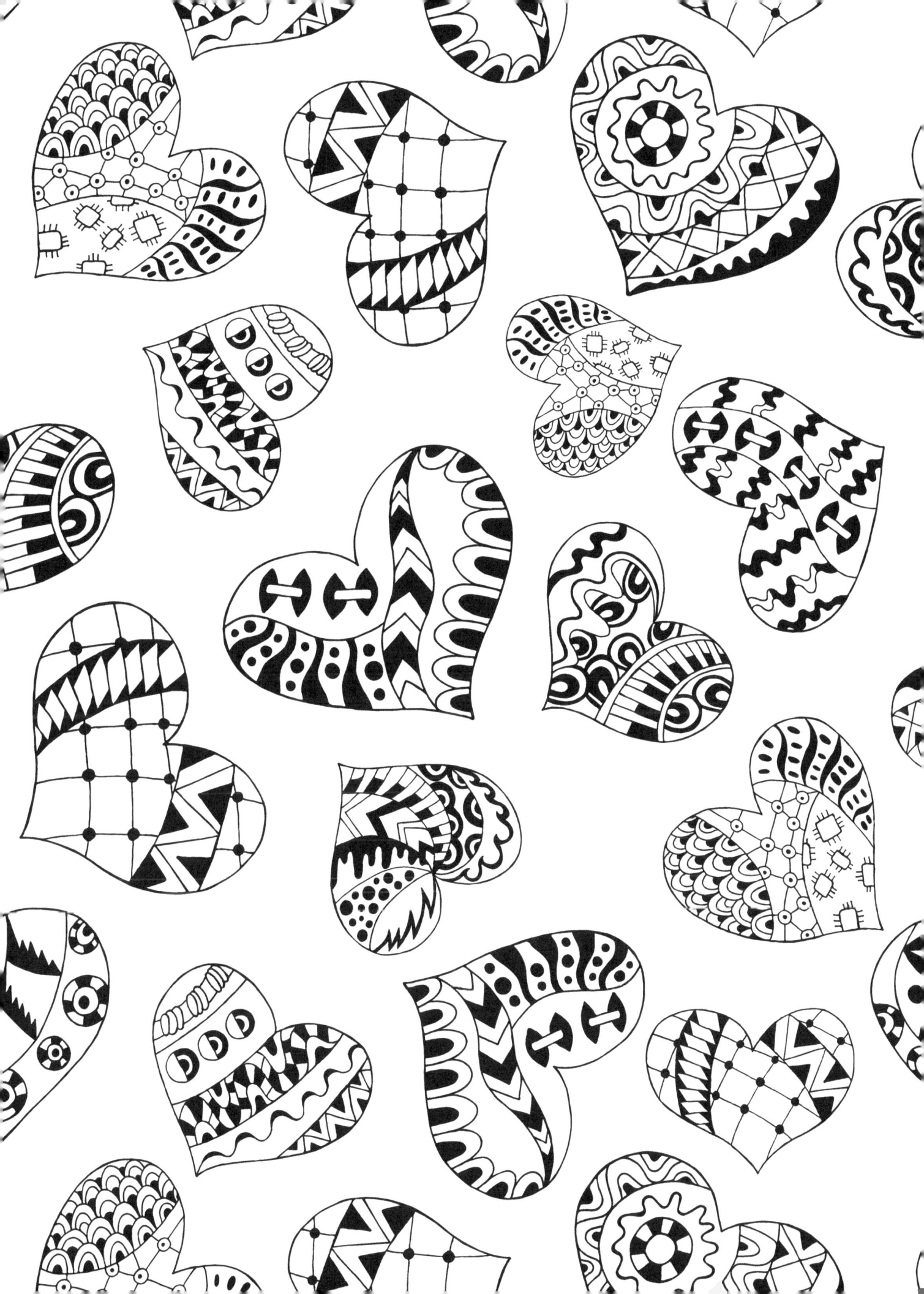

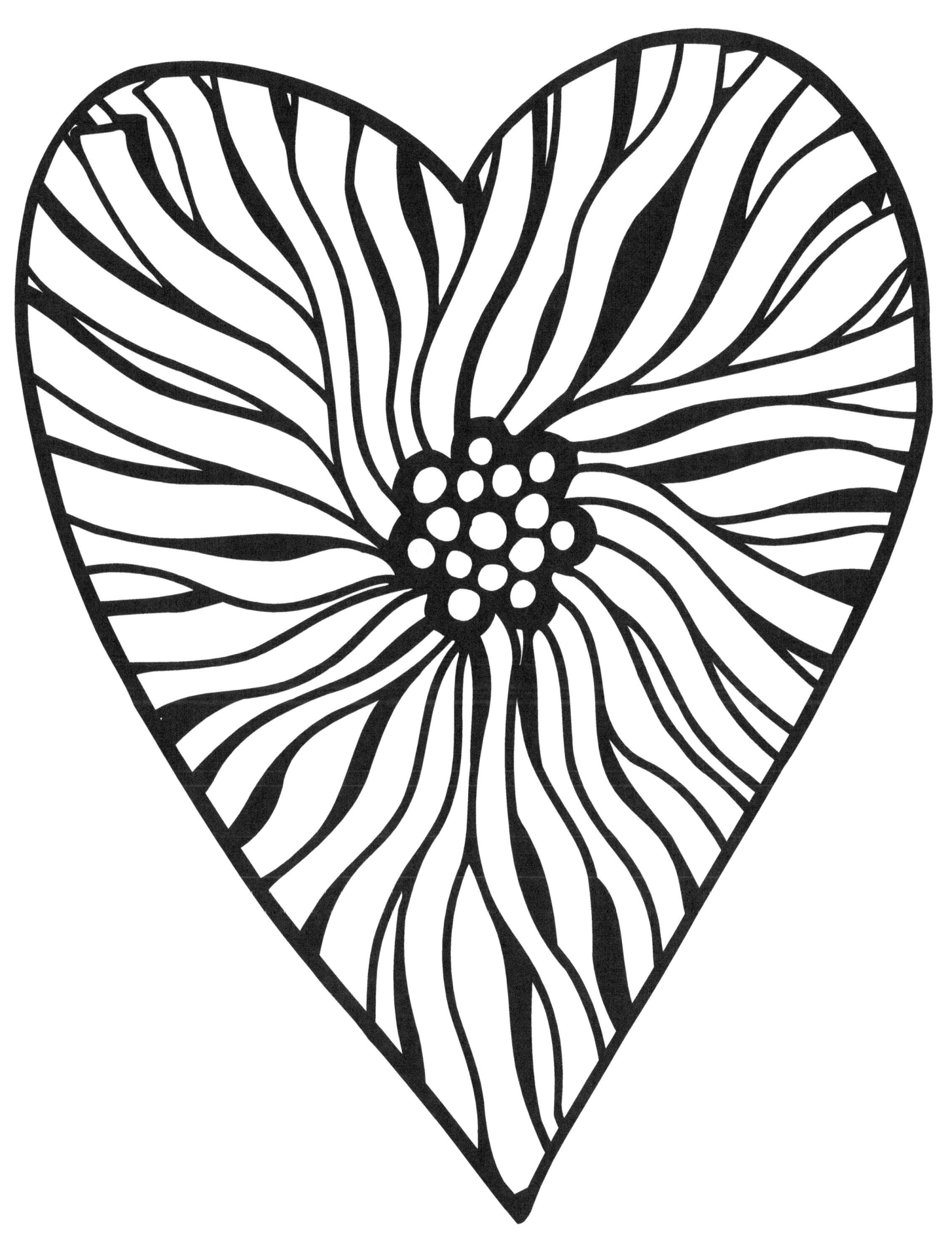

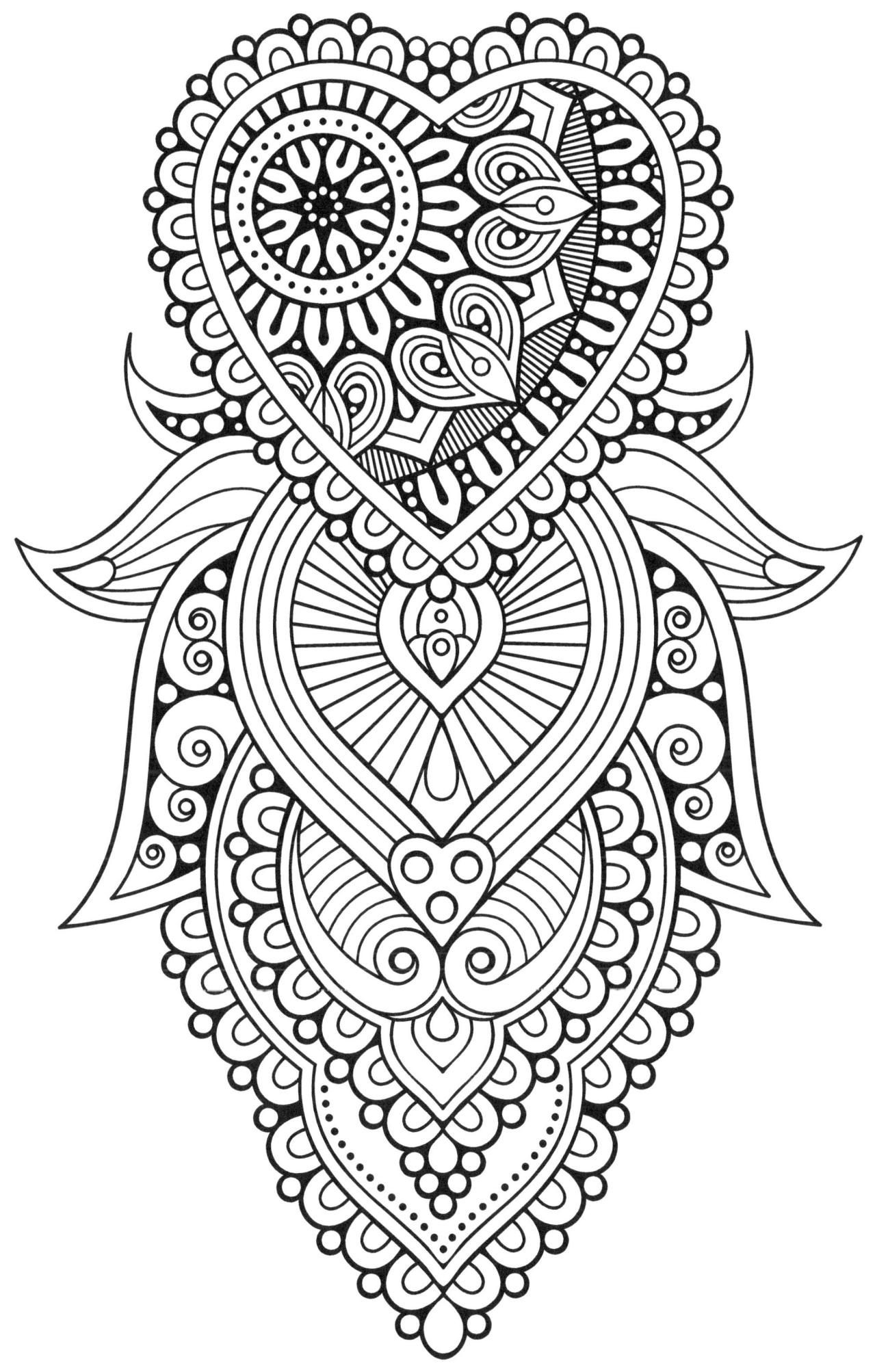

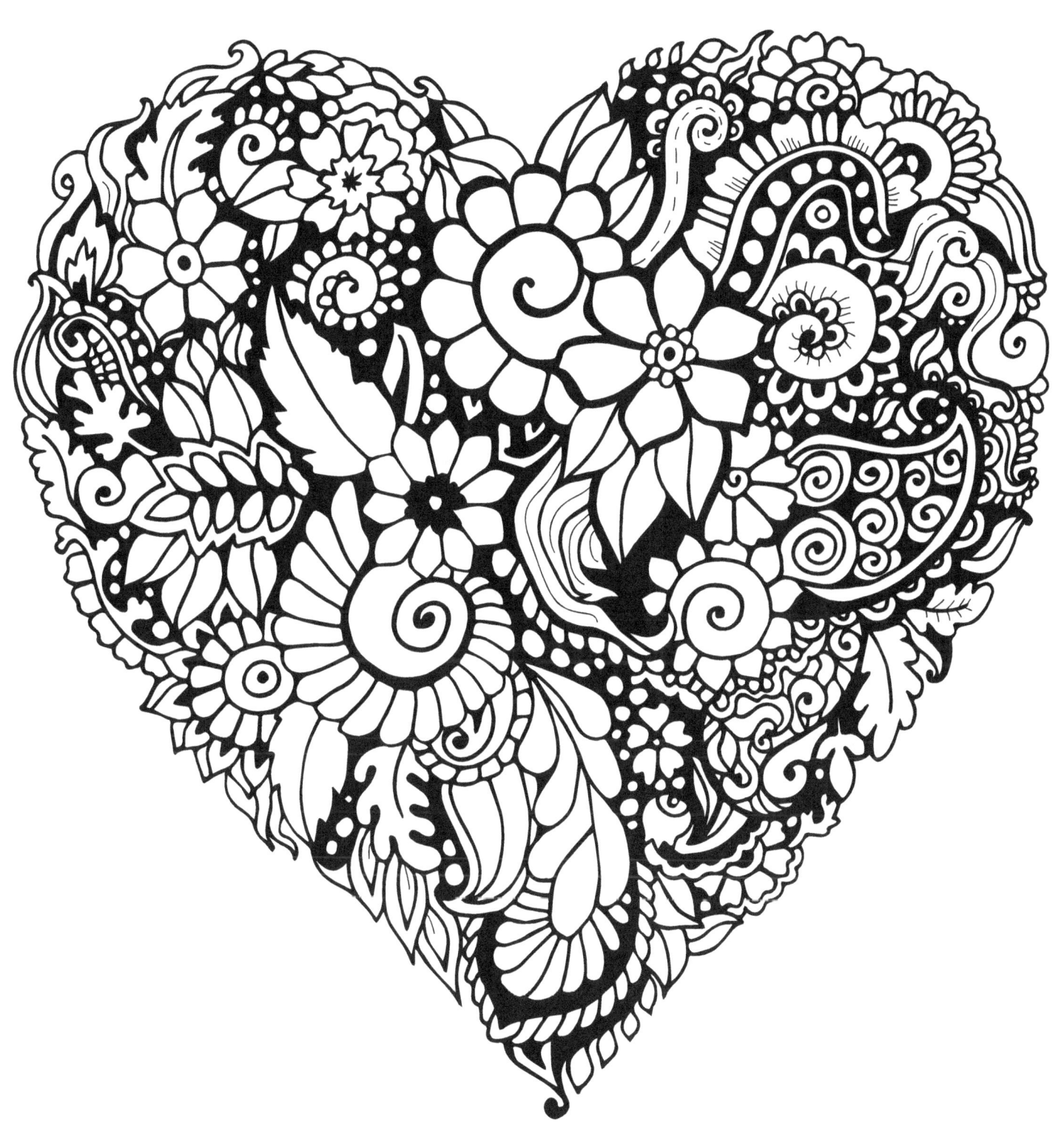

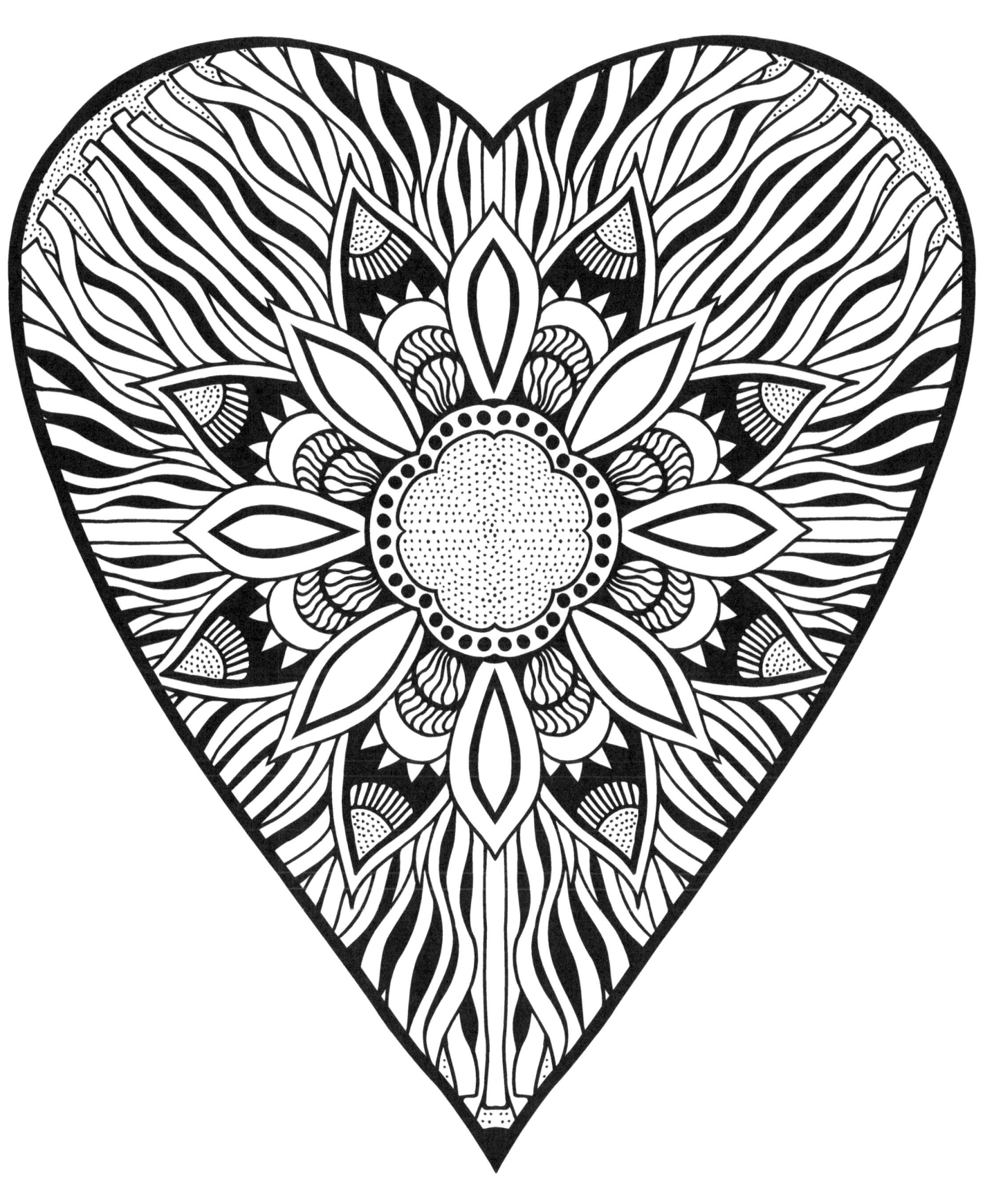

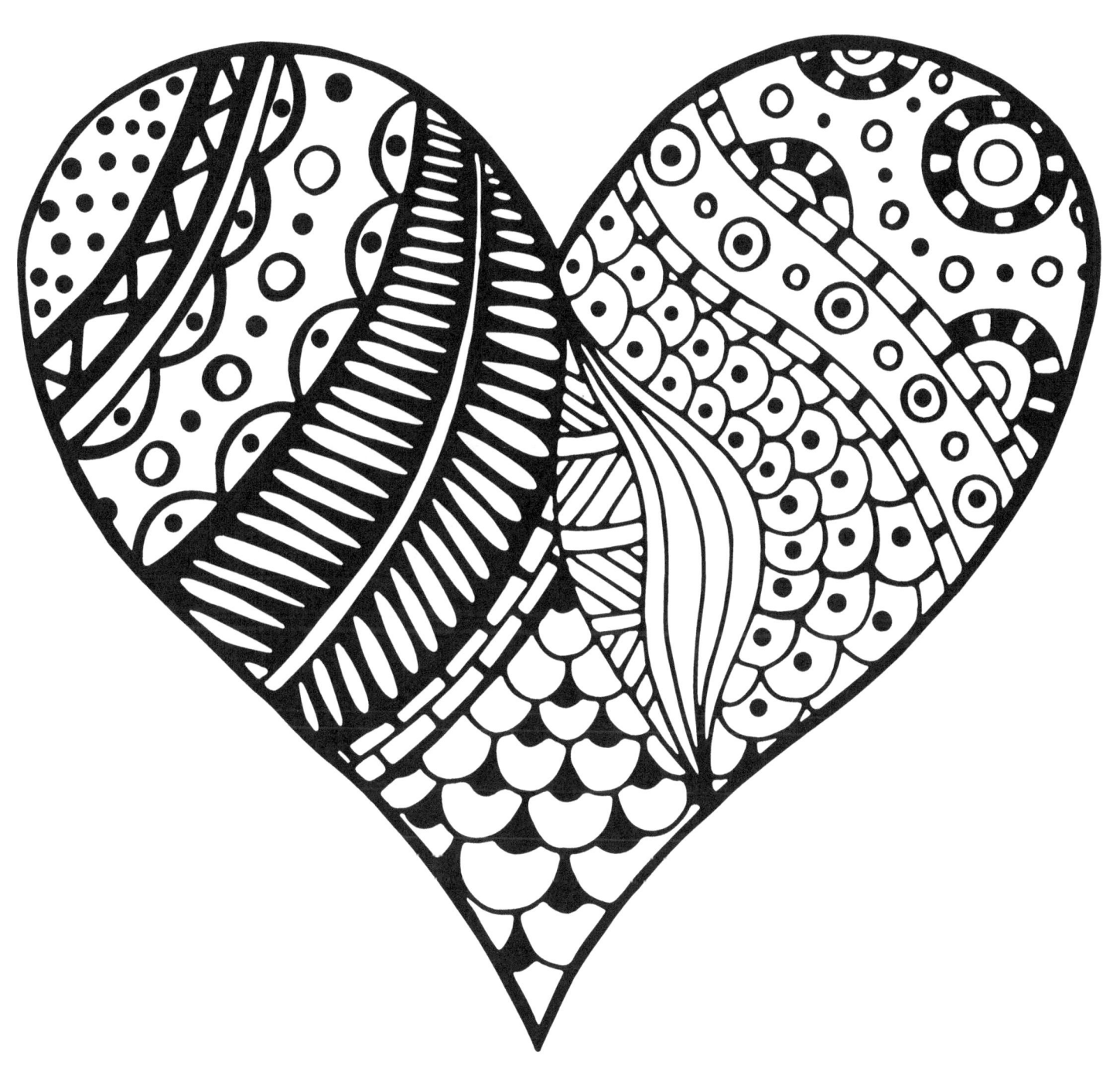

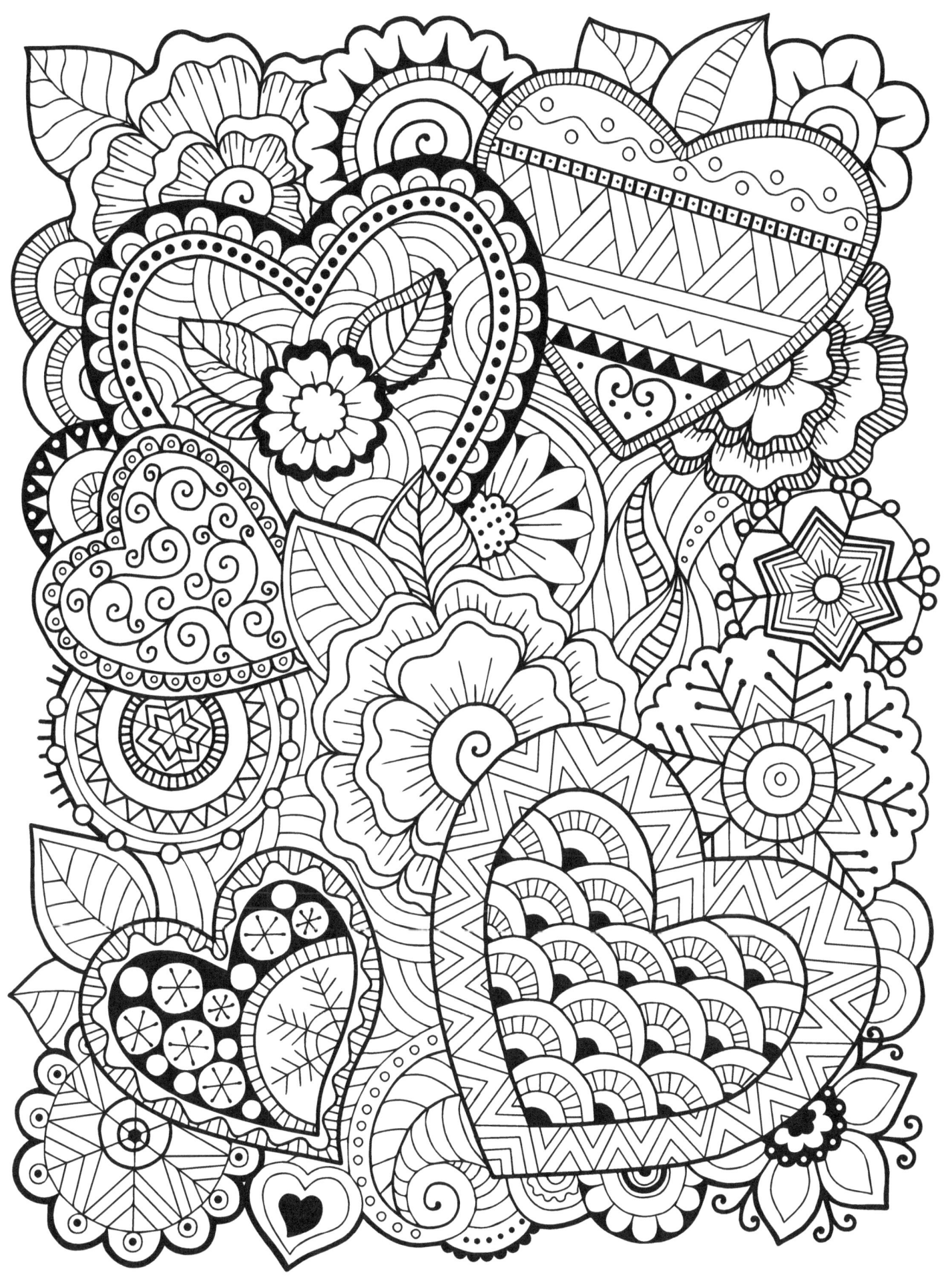

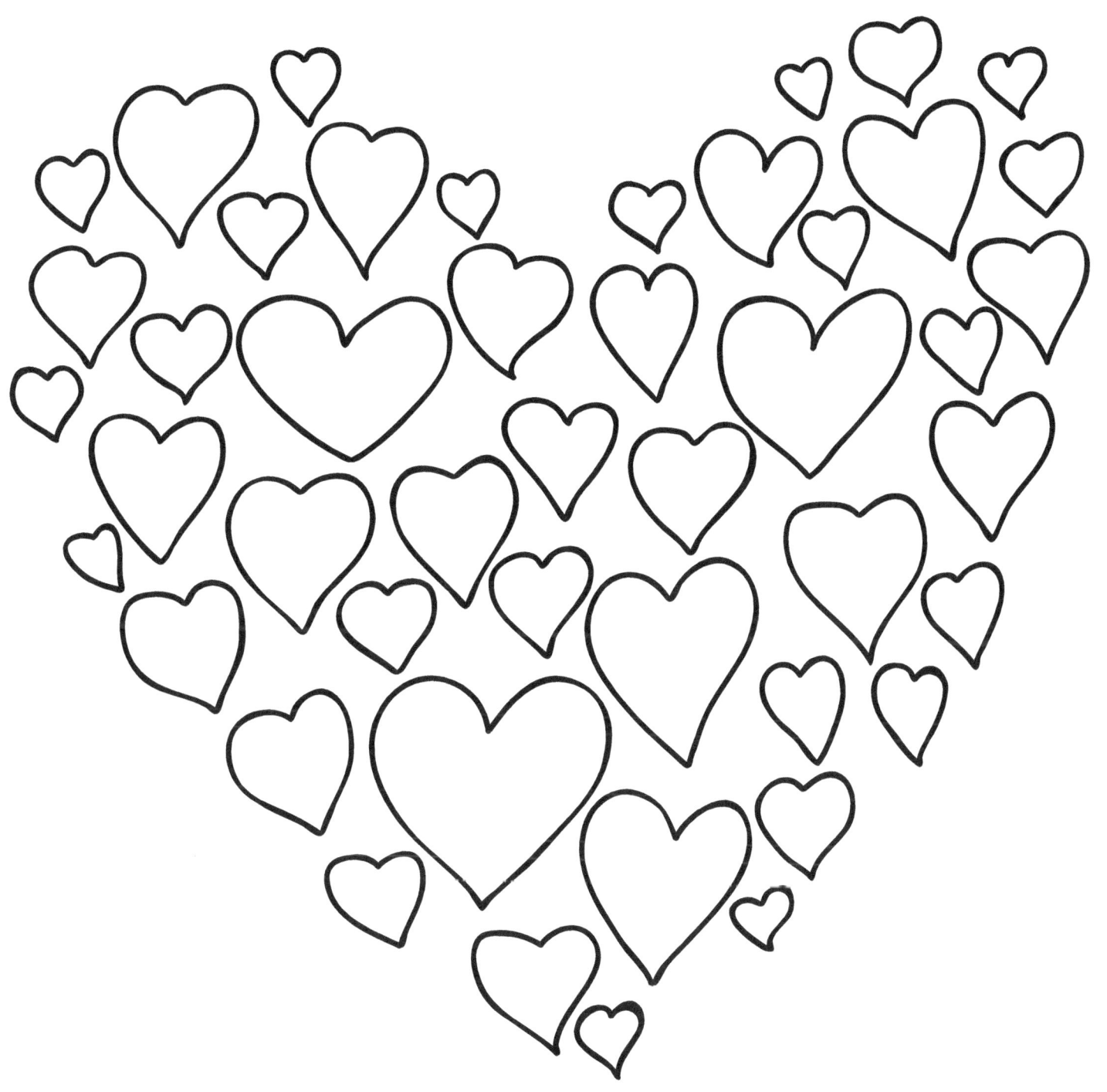

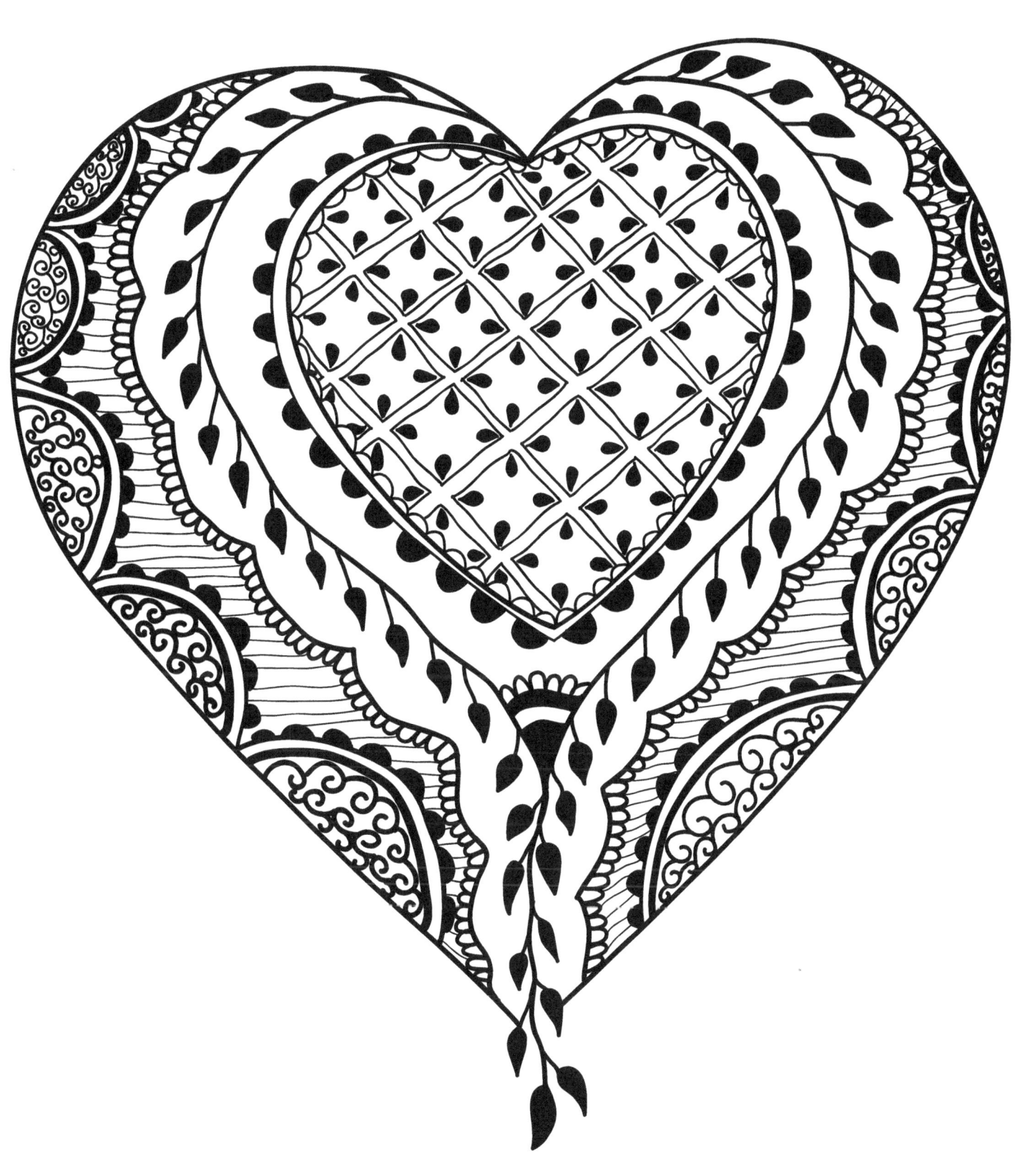

.

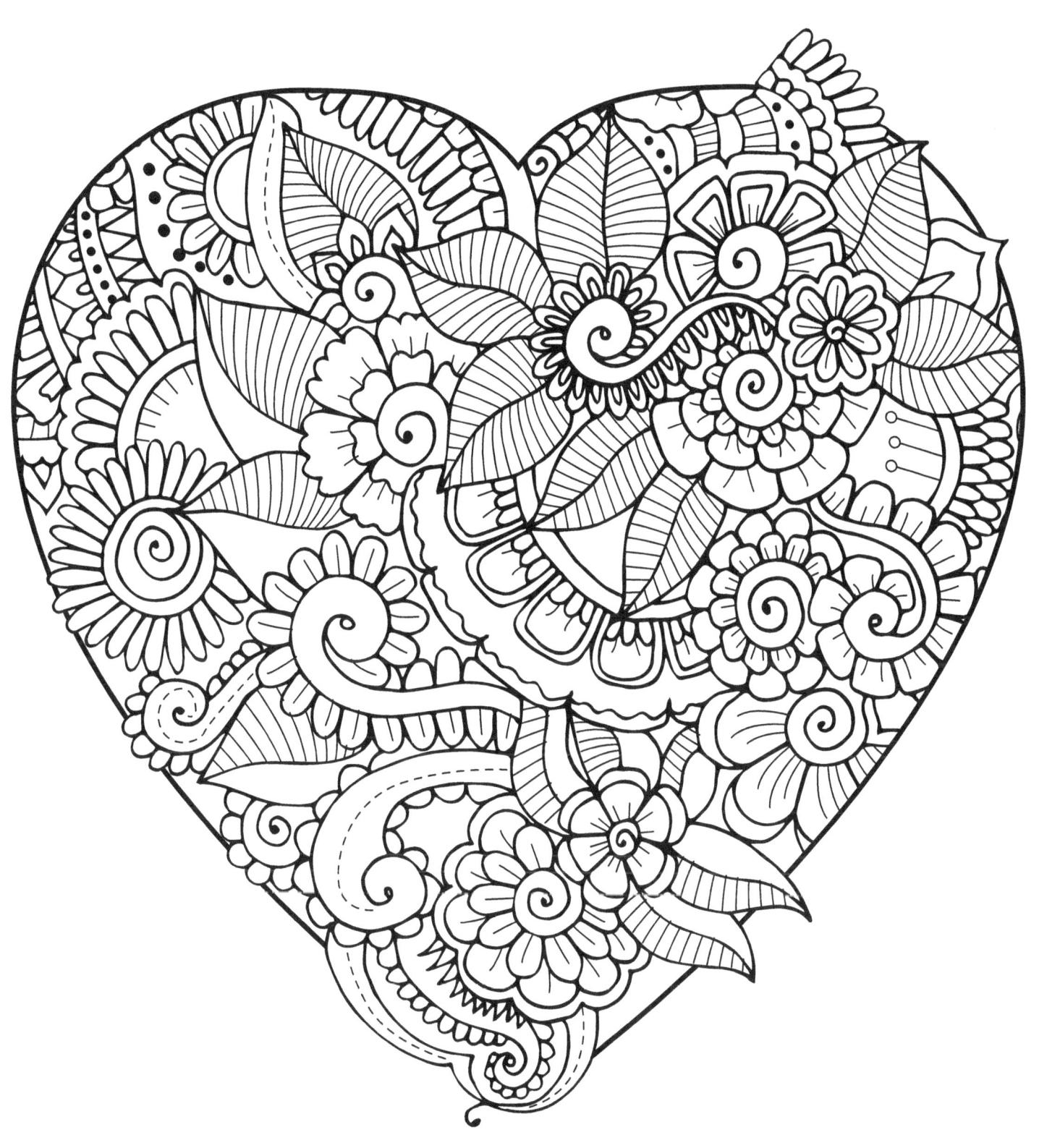

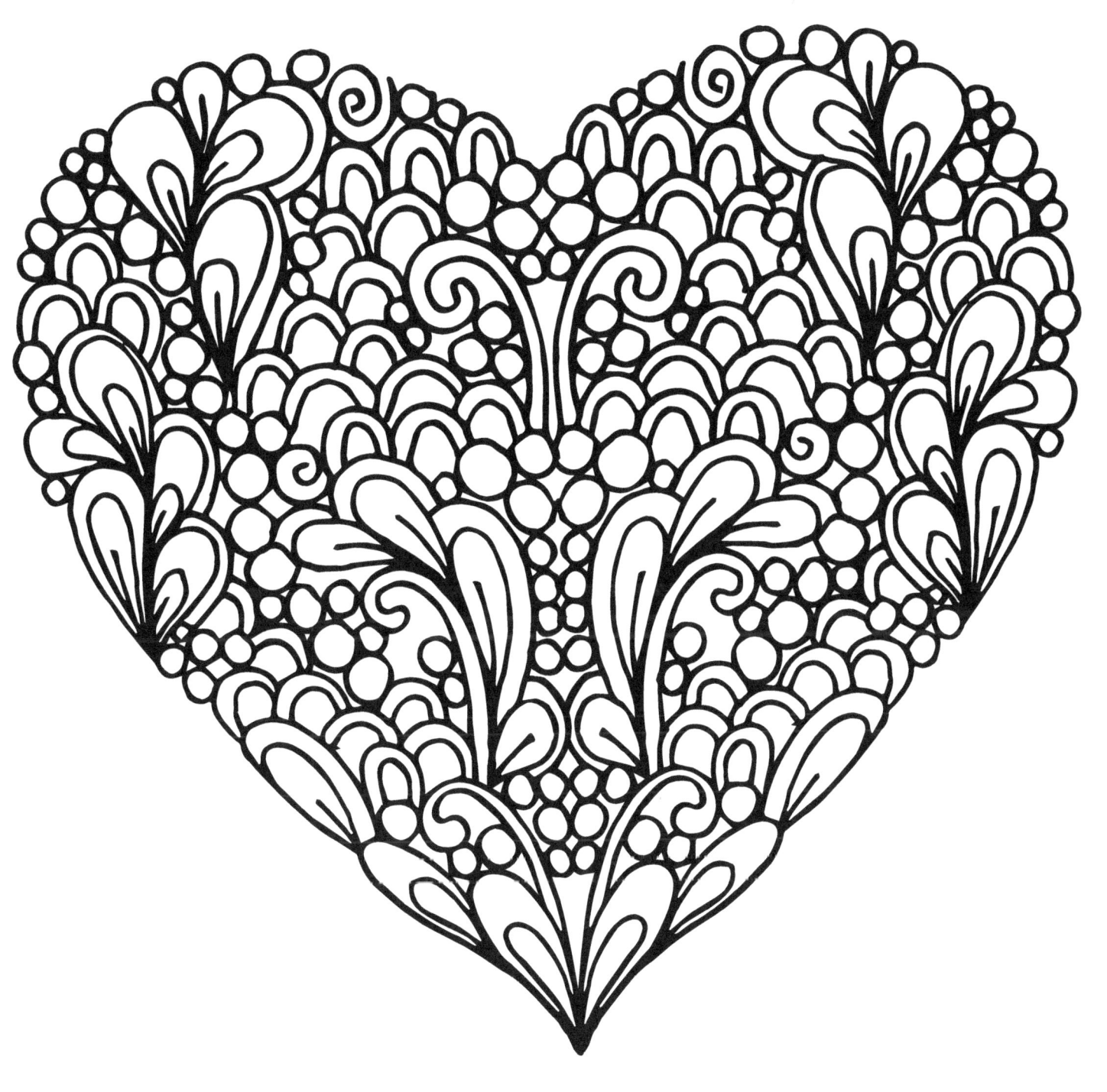

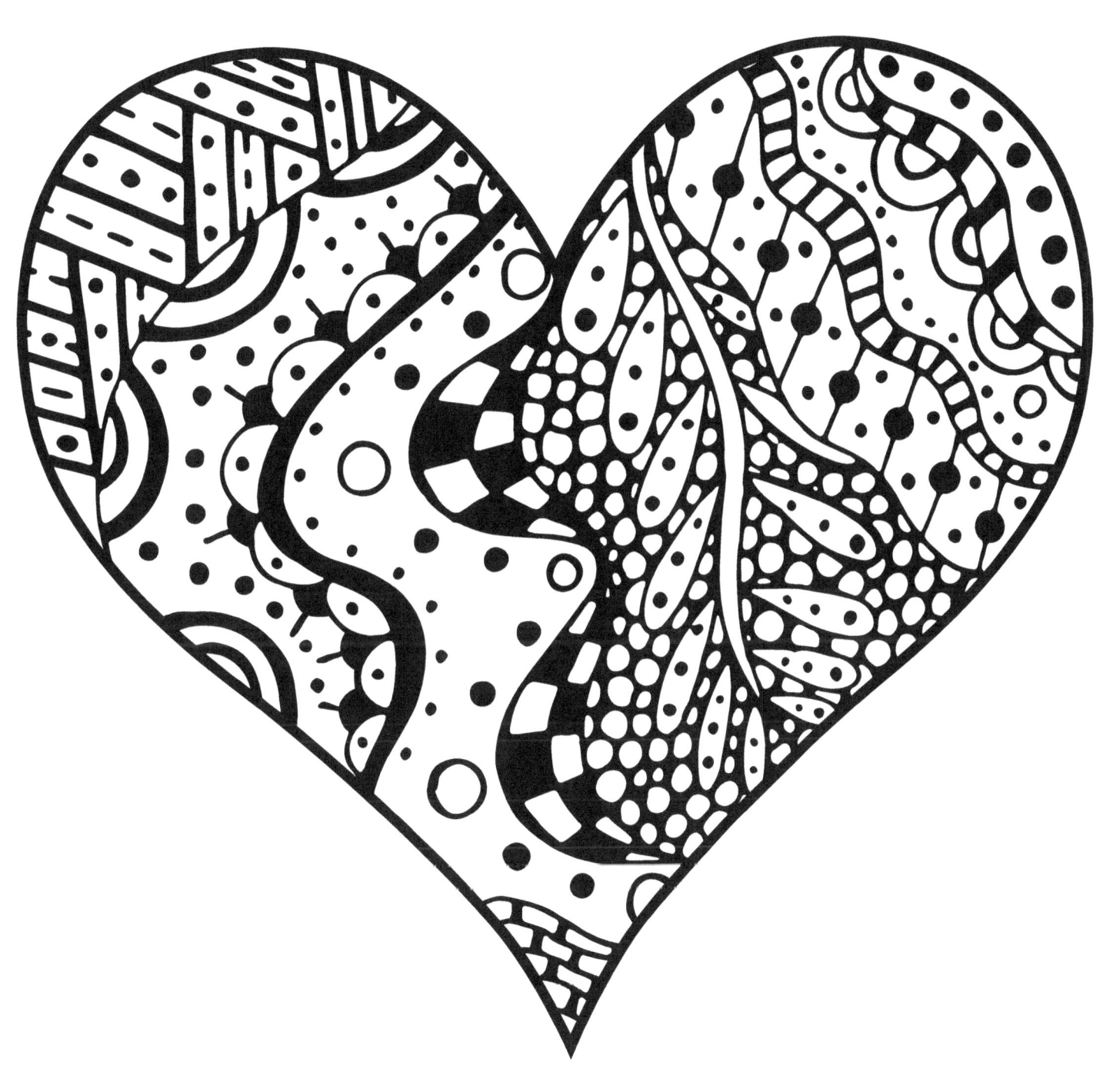

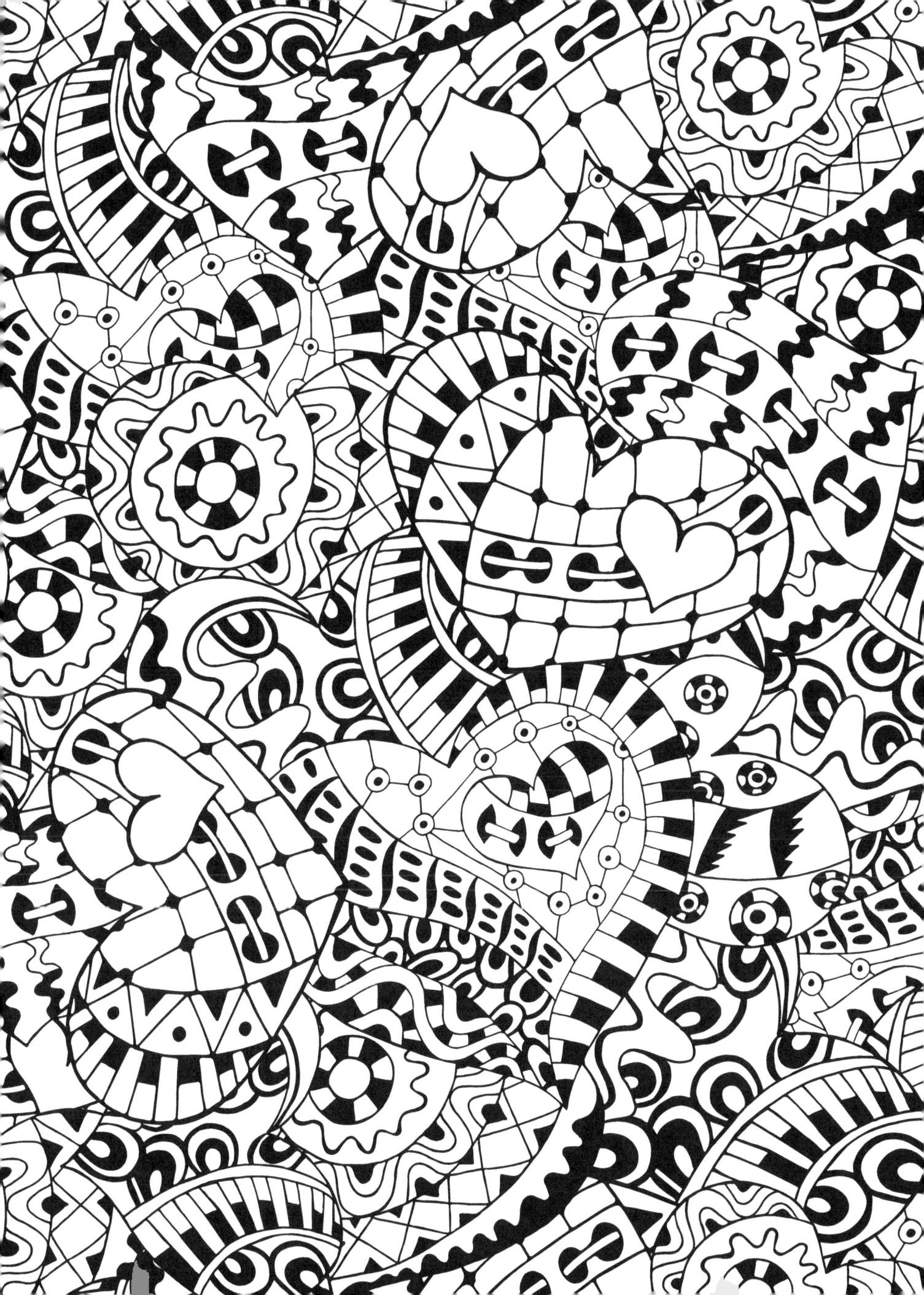

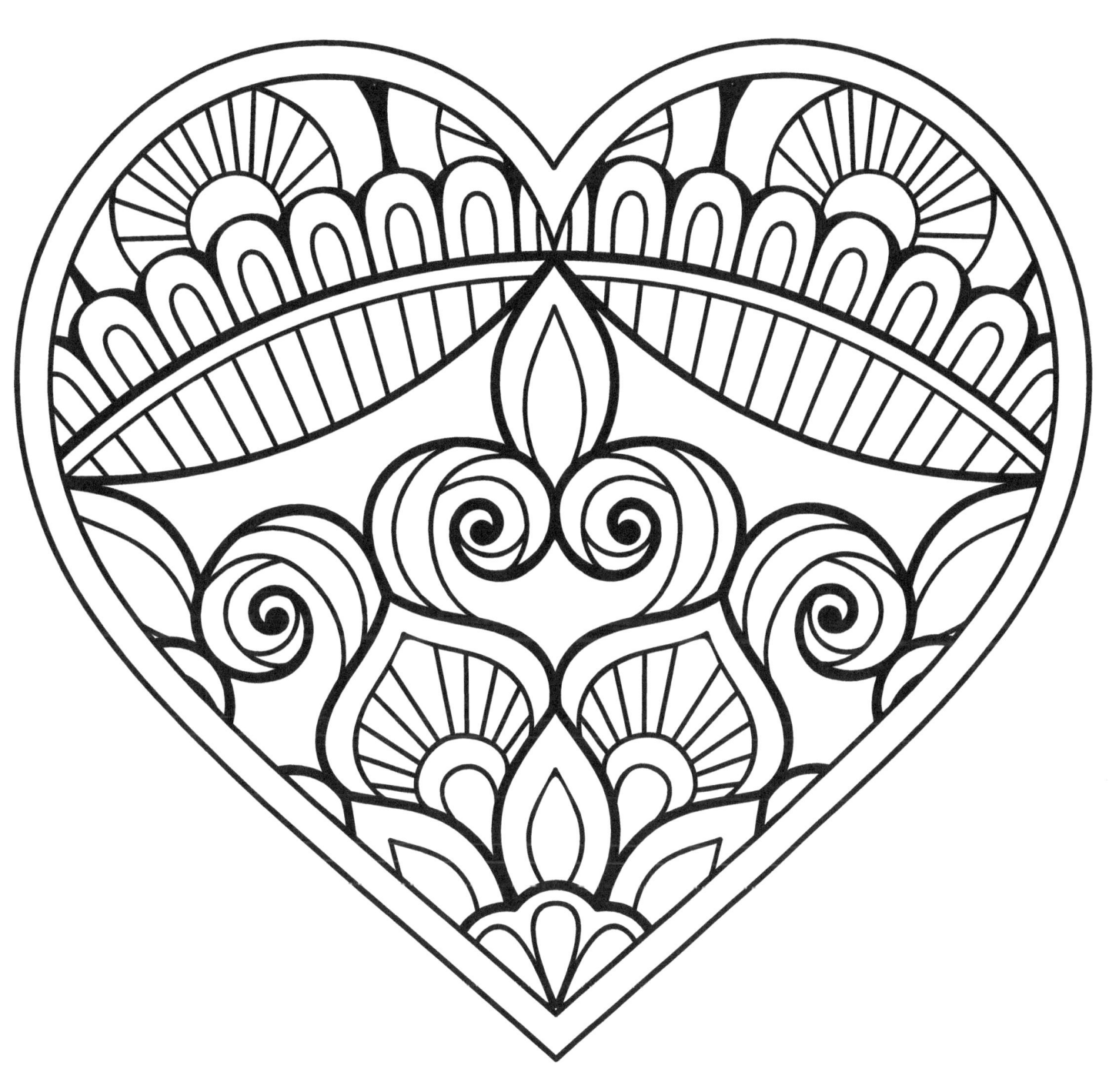

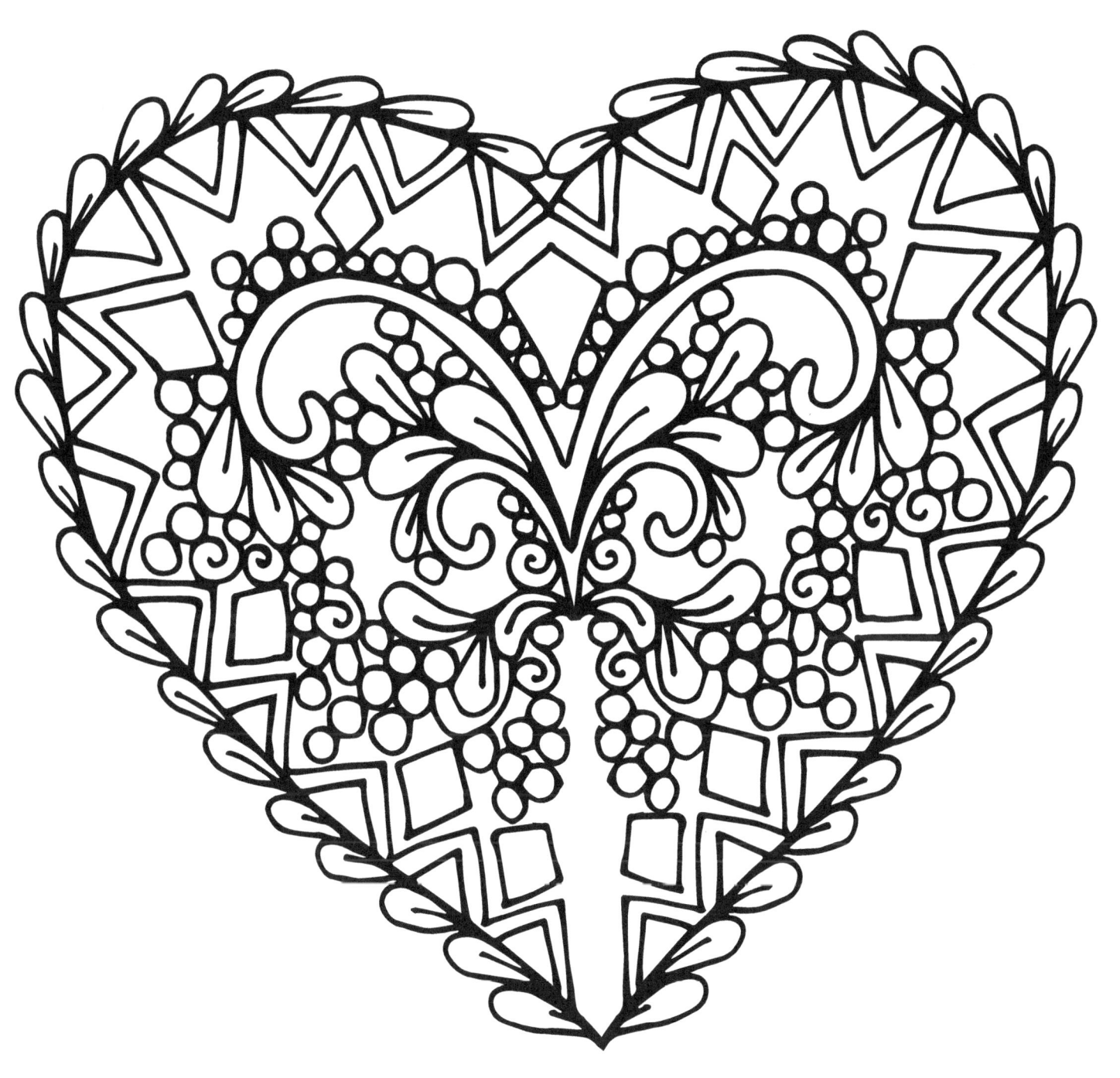

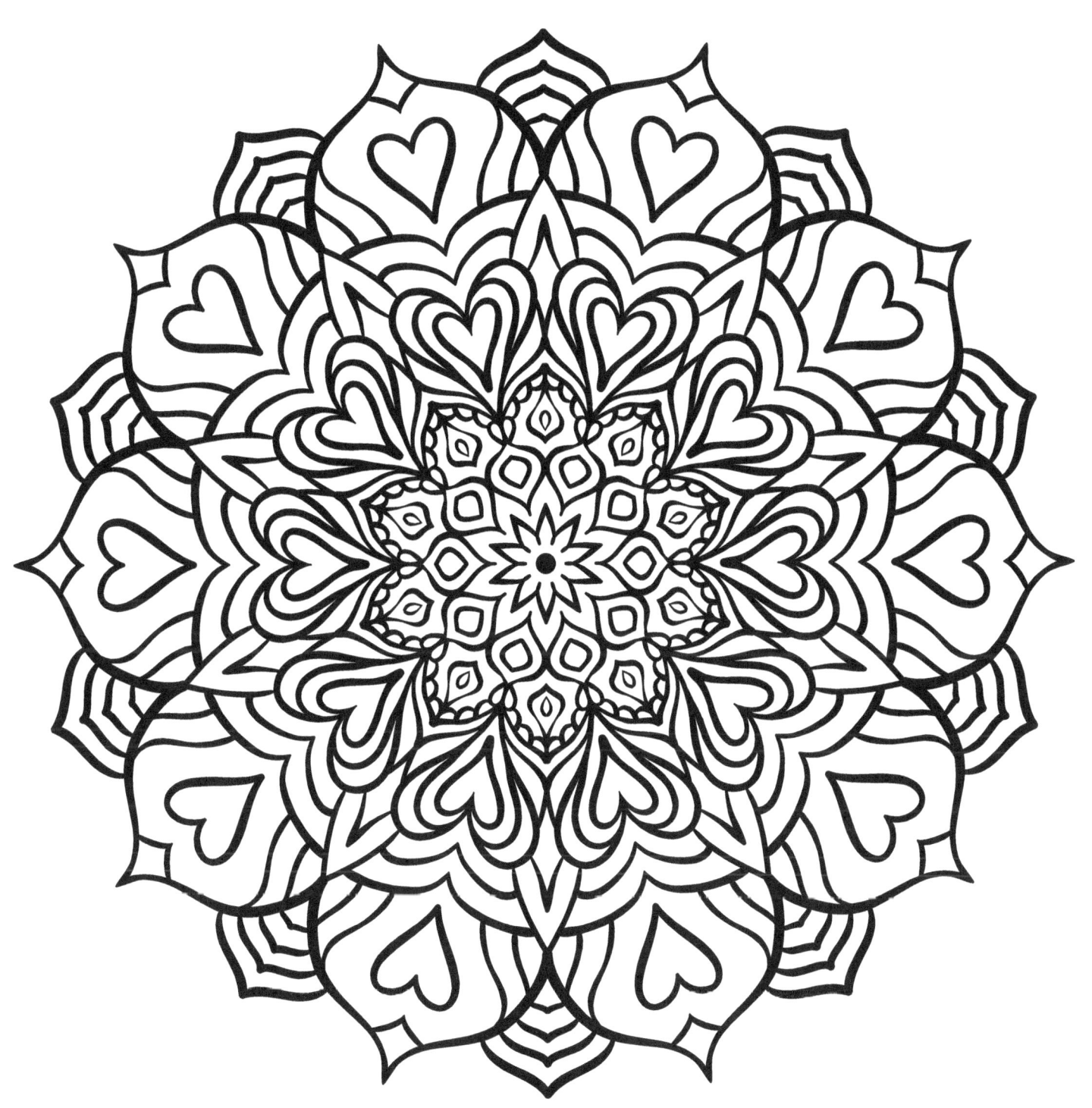

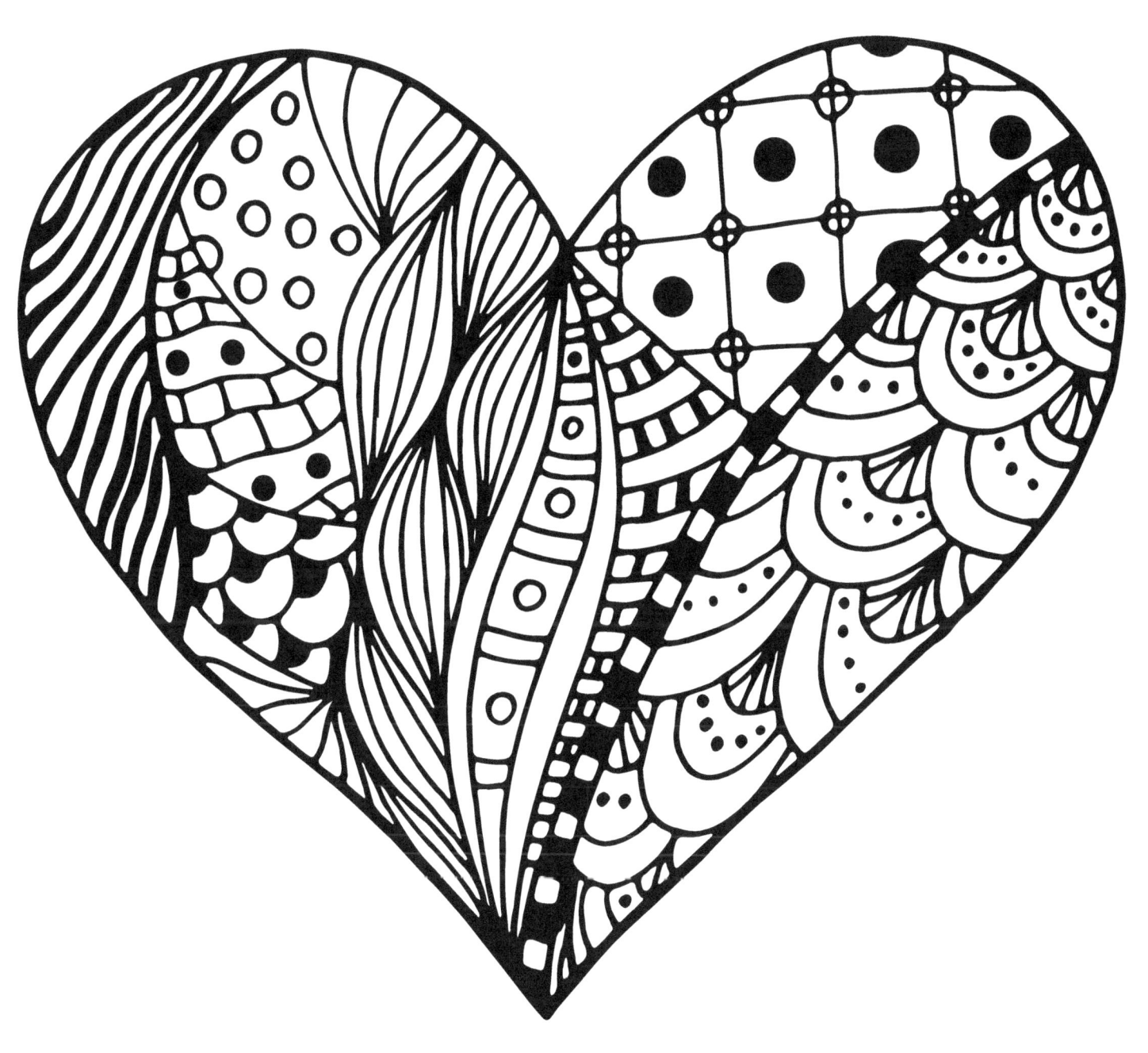

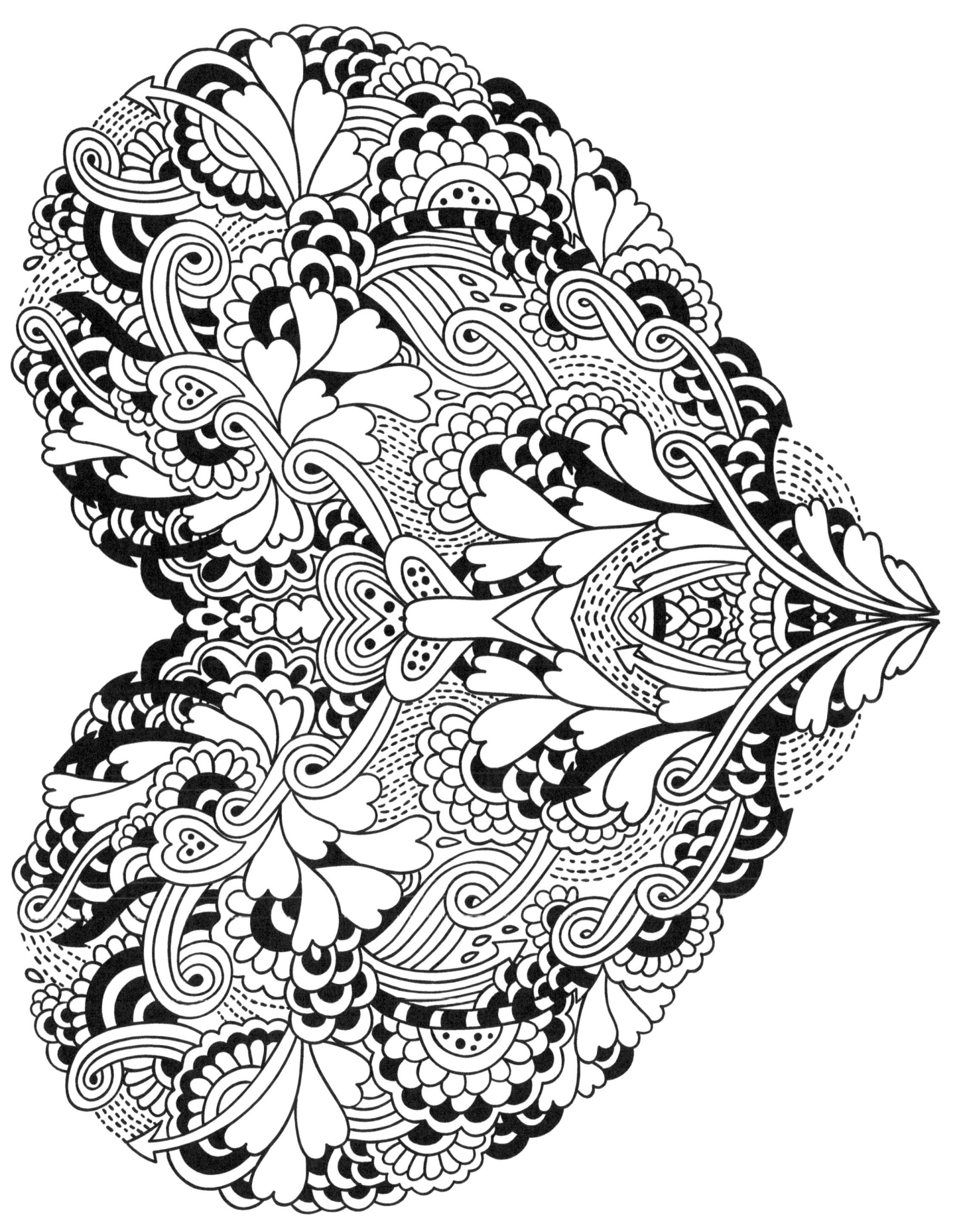

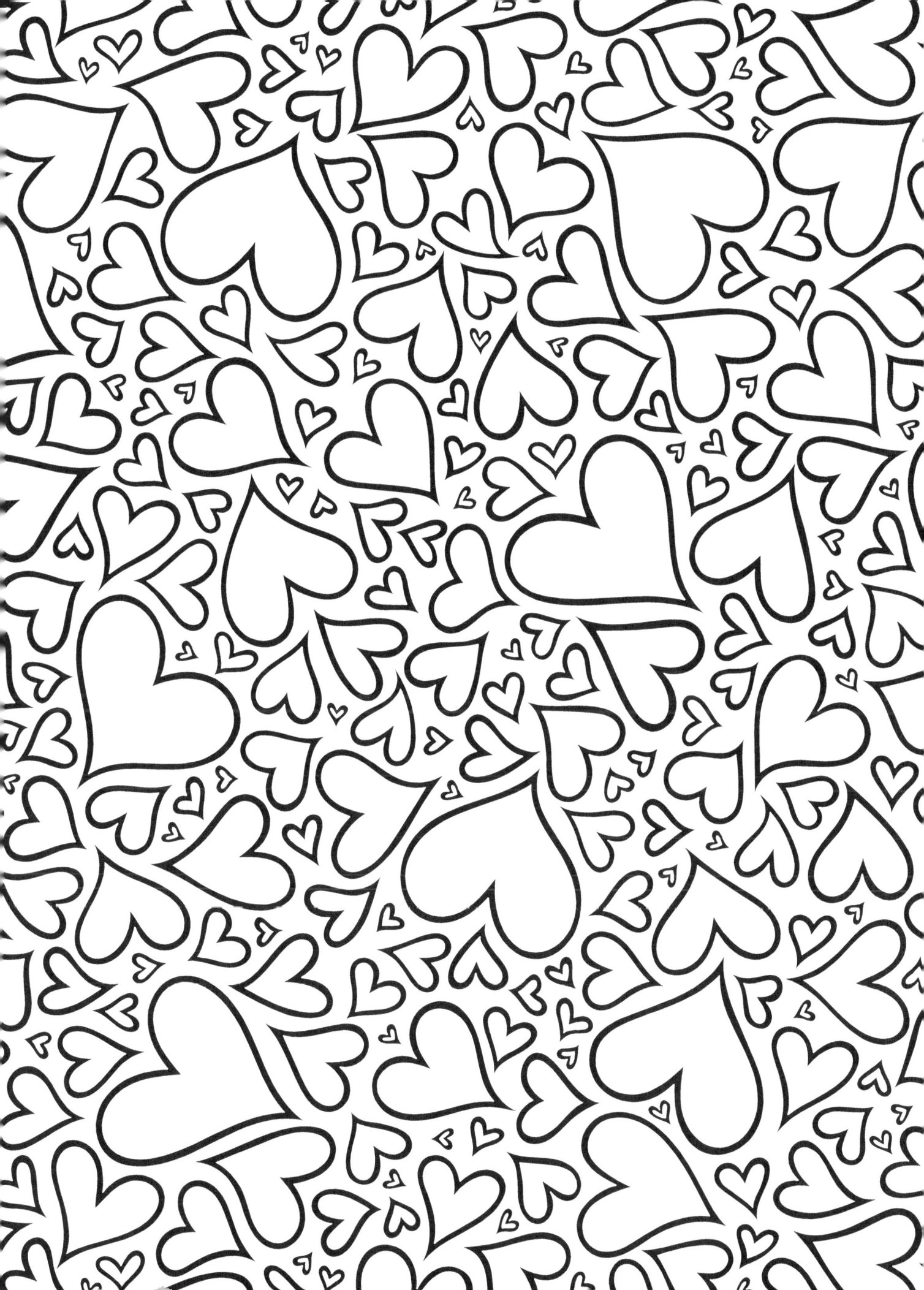

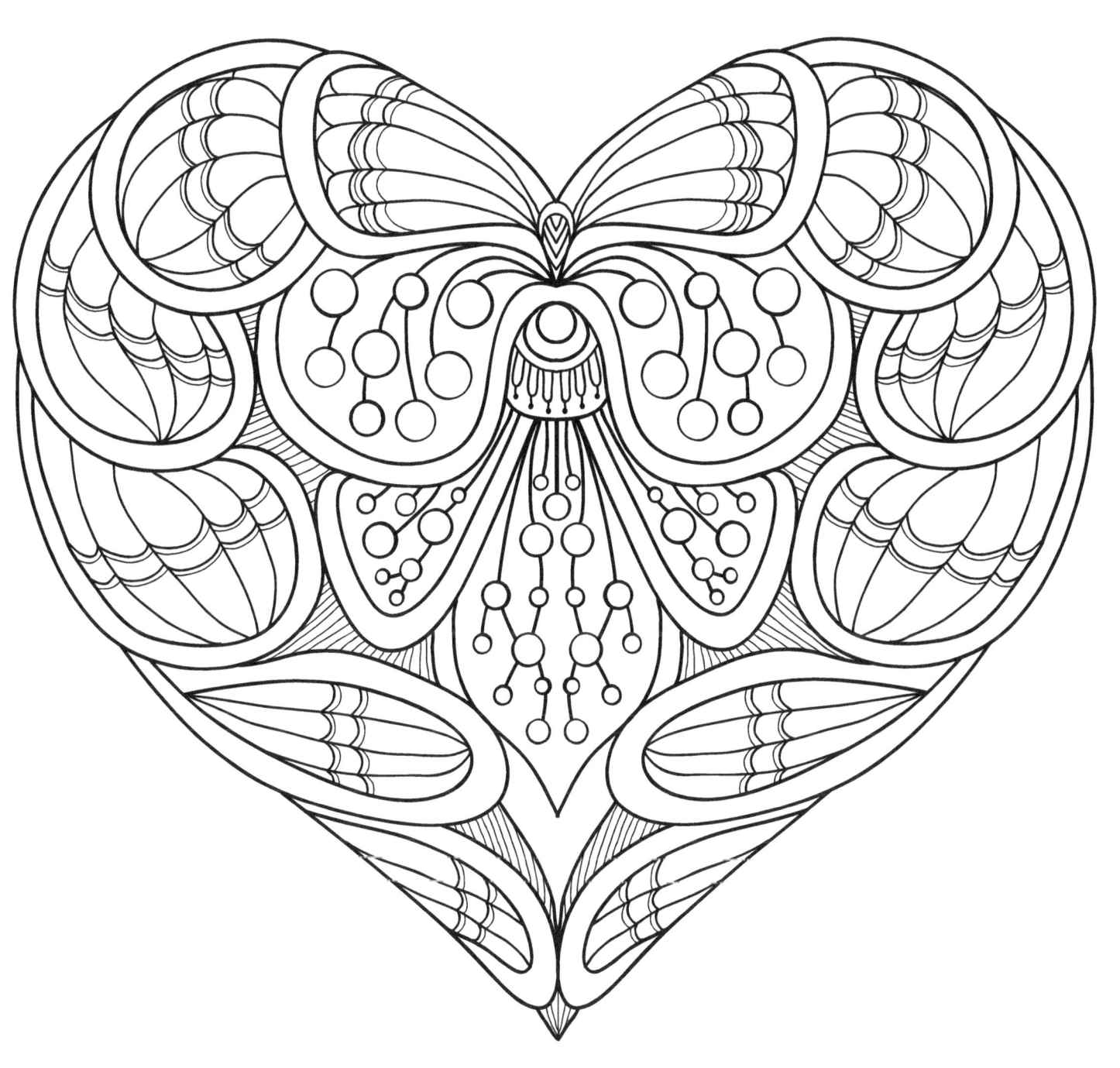

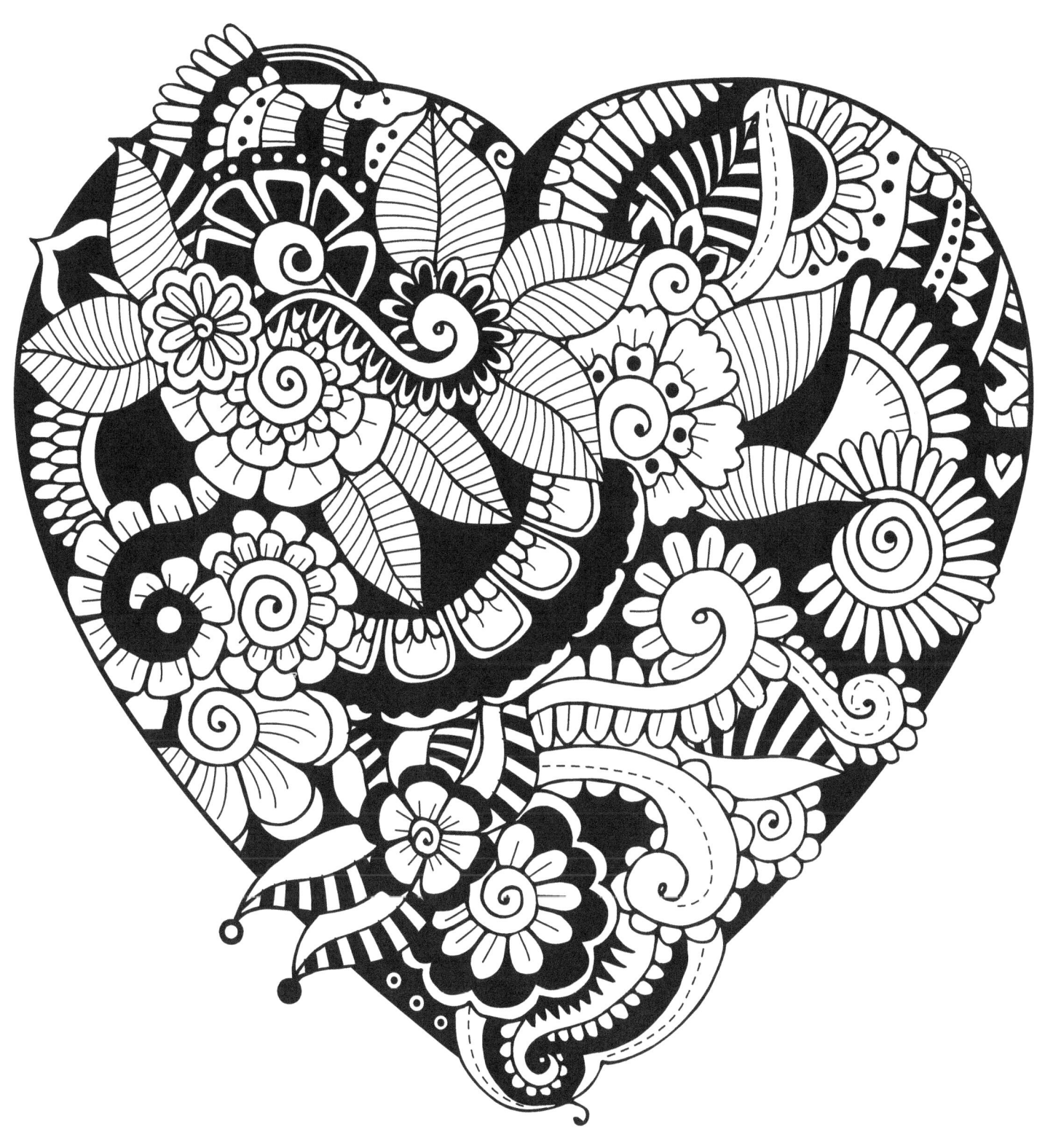

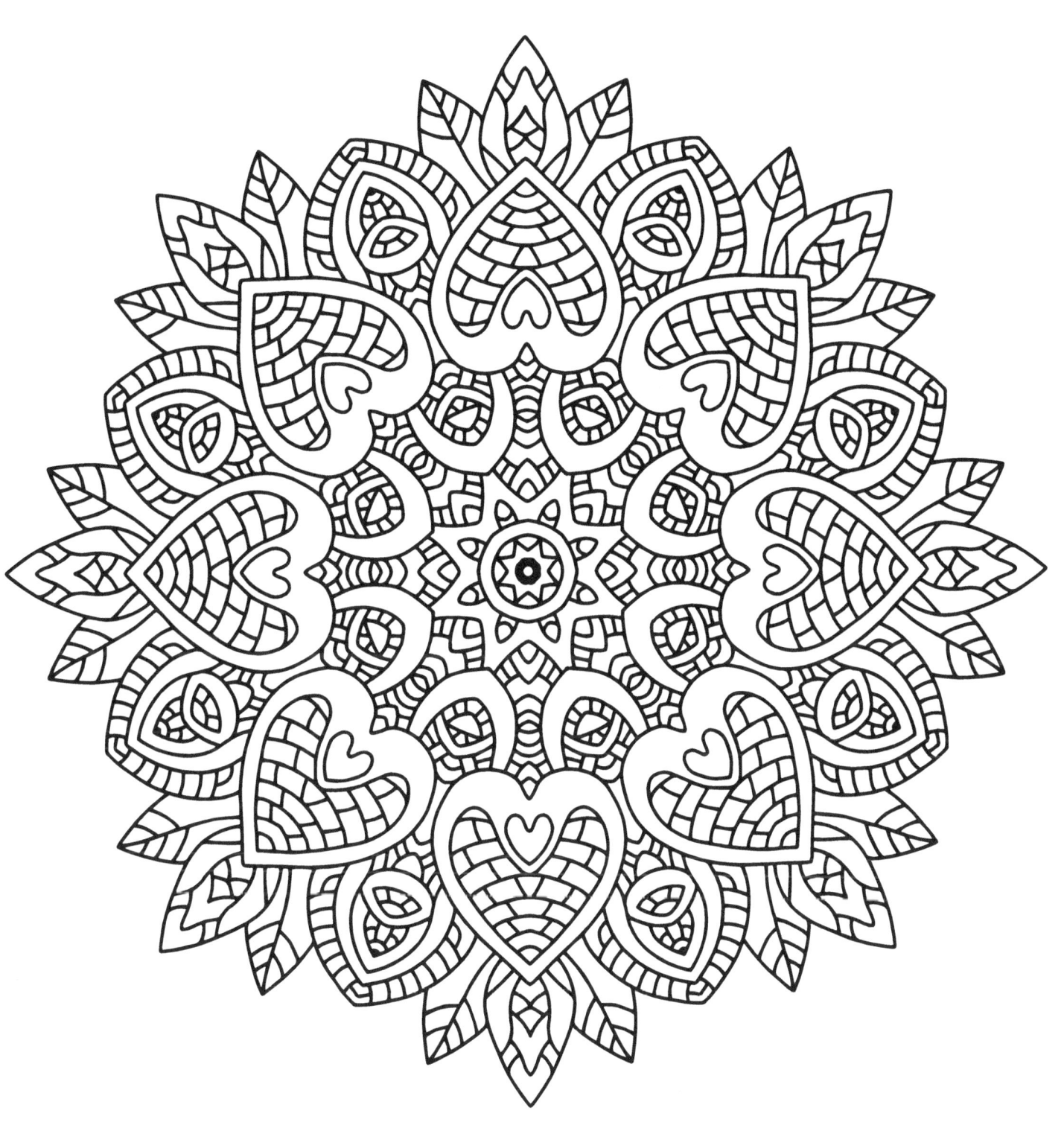

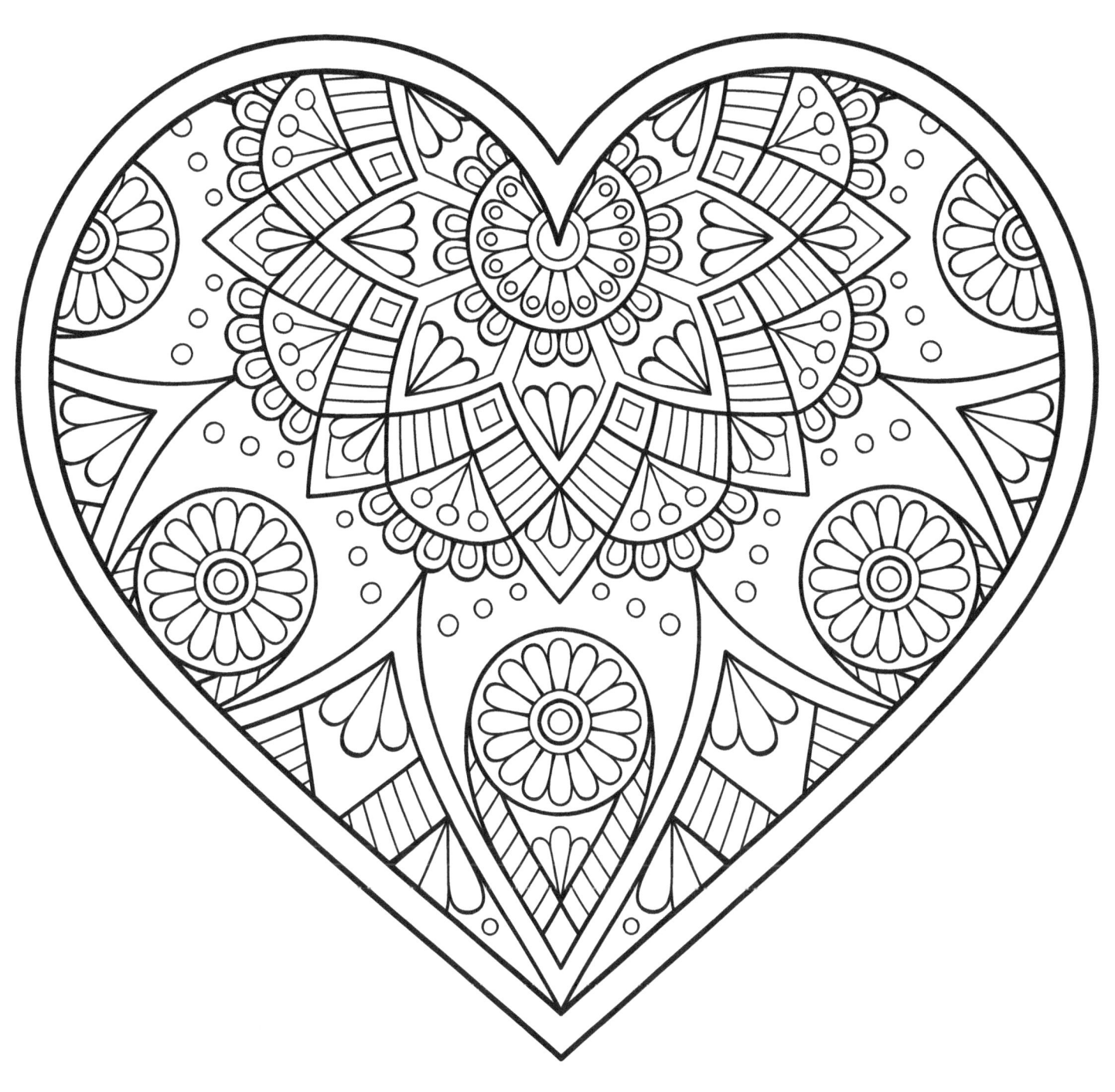

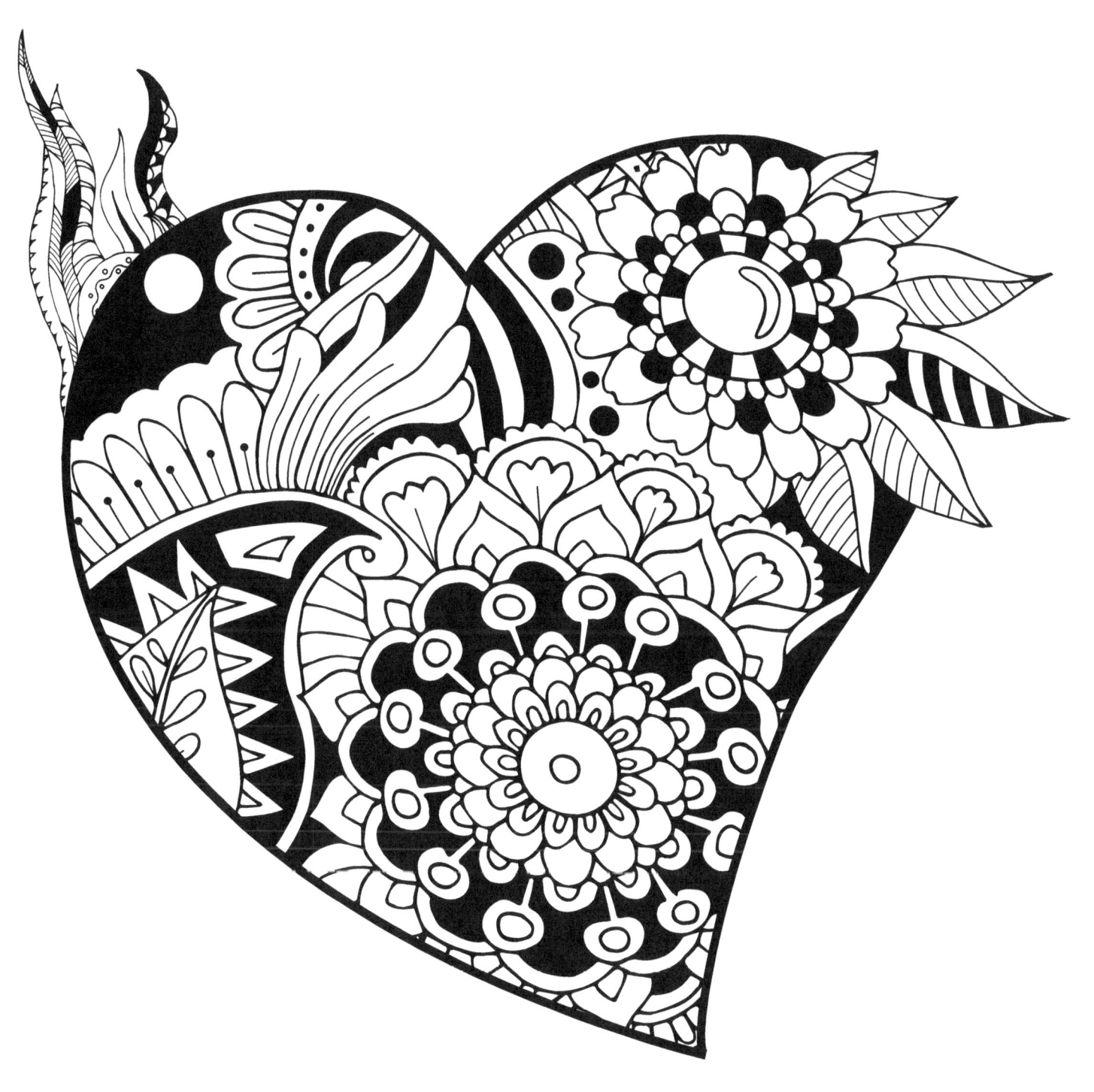

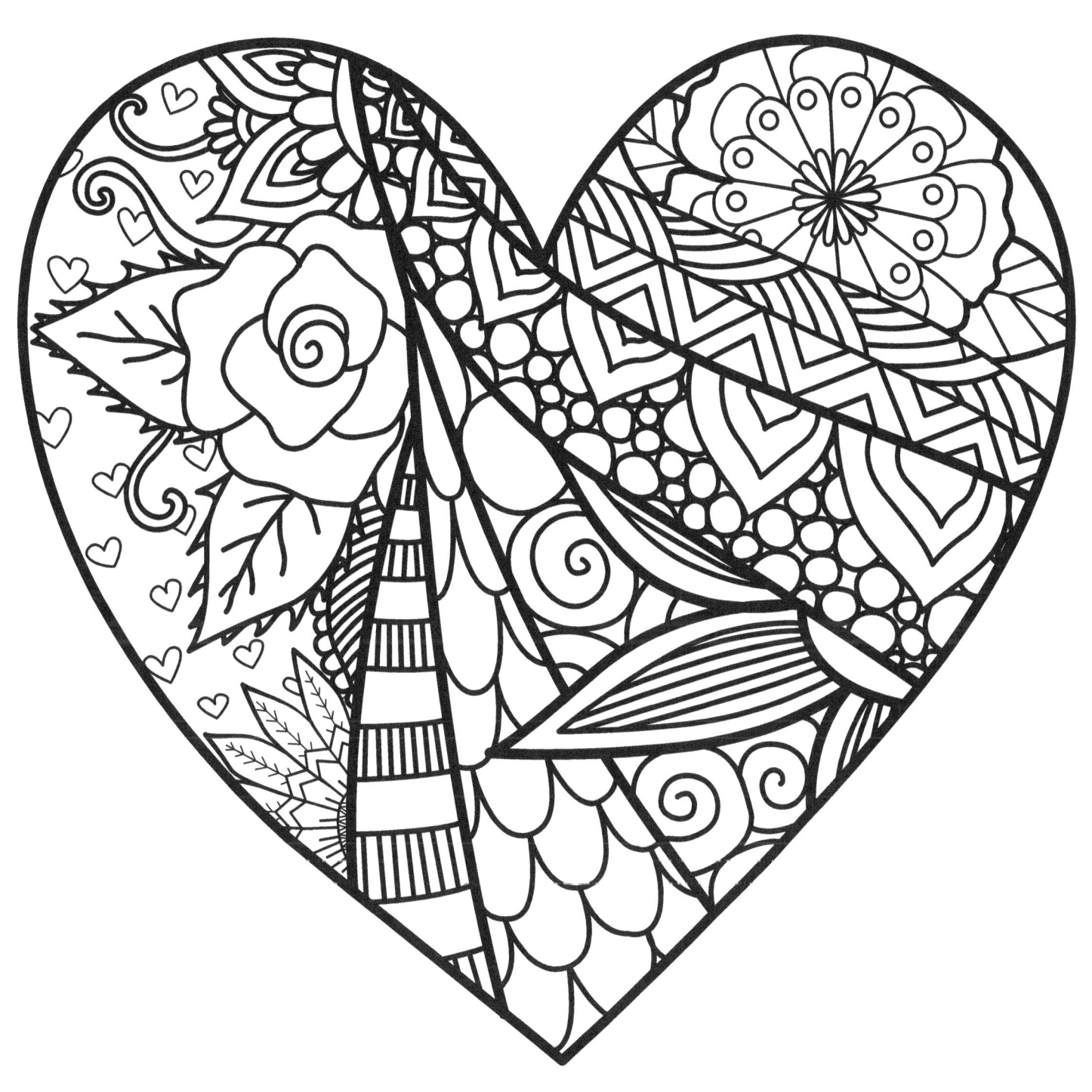

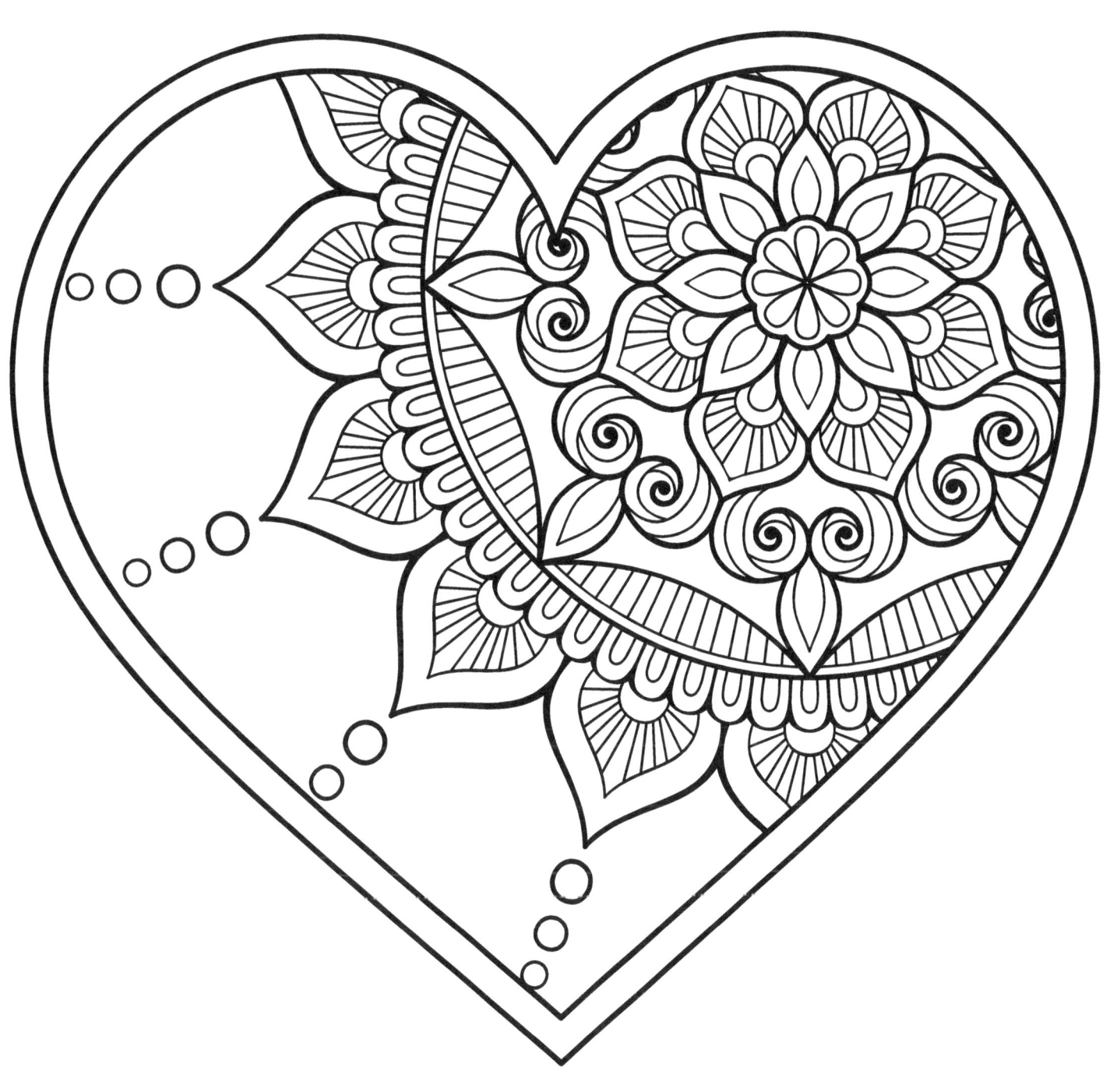

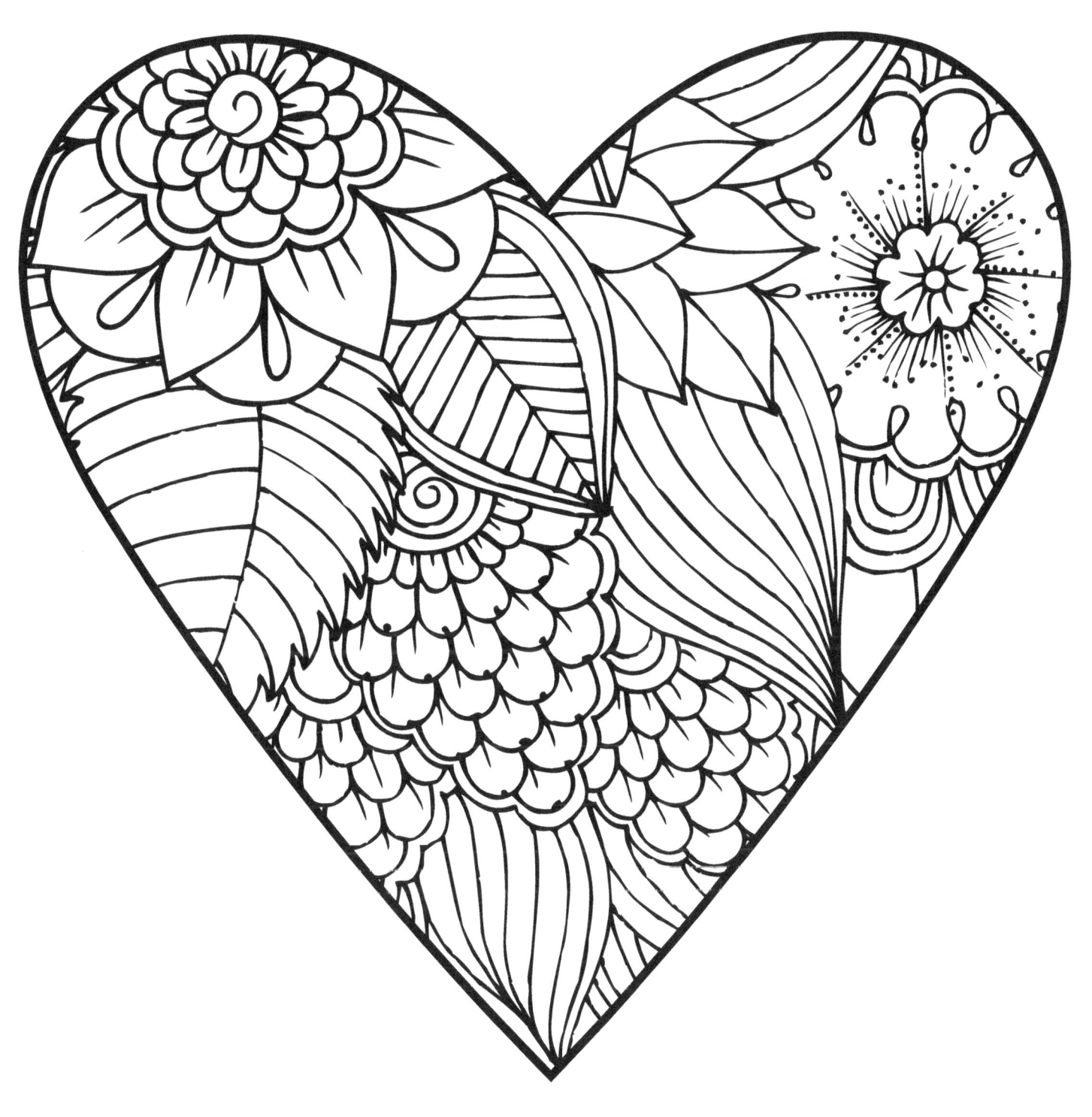

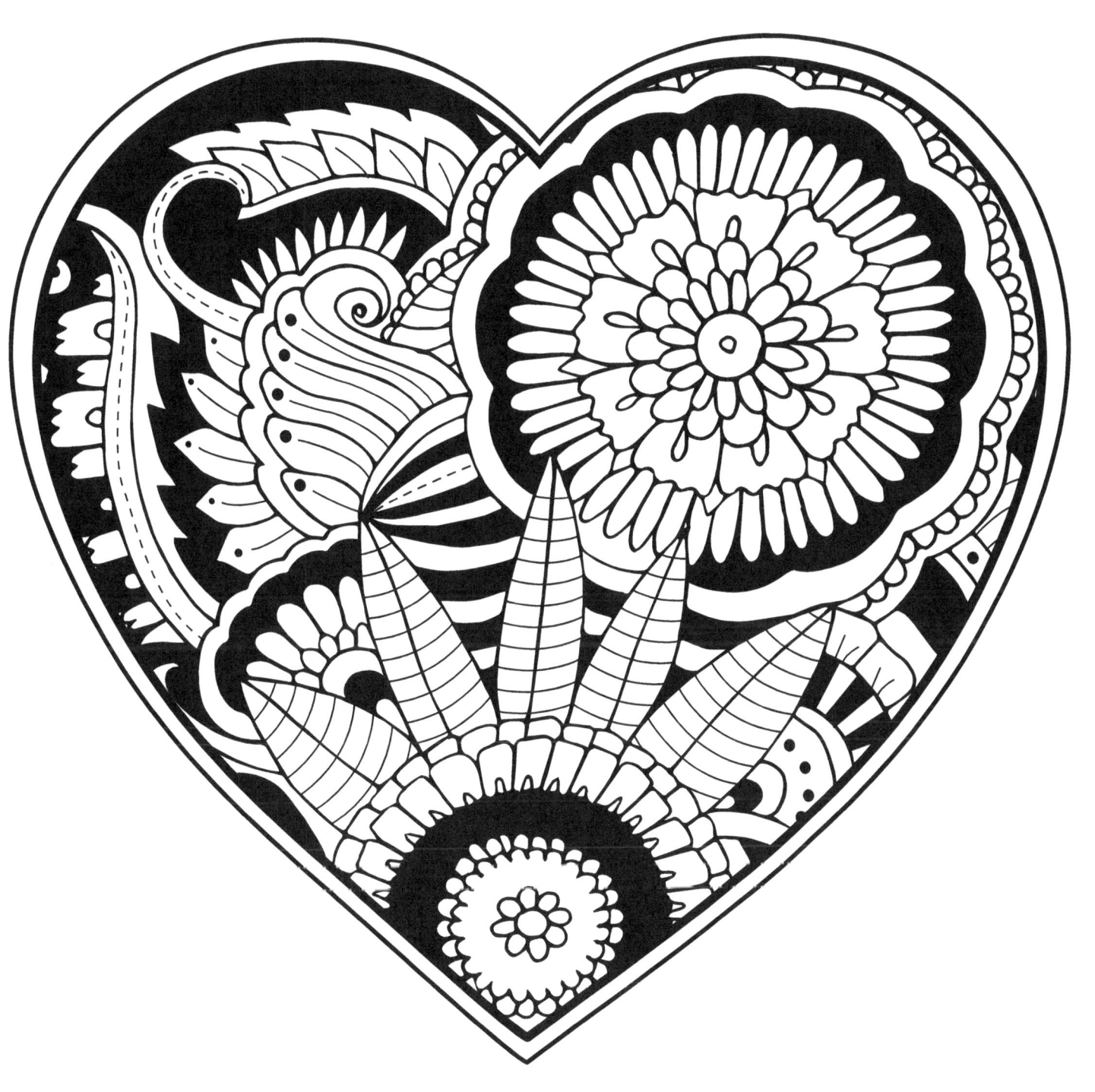

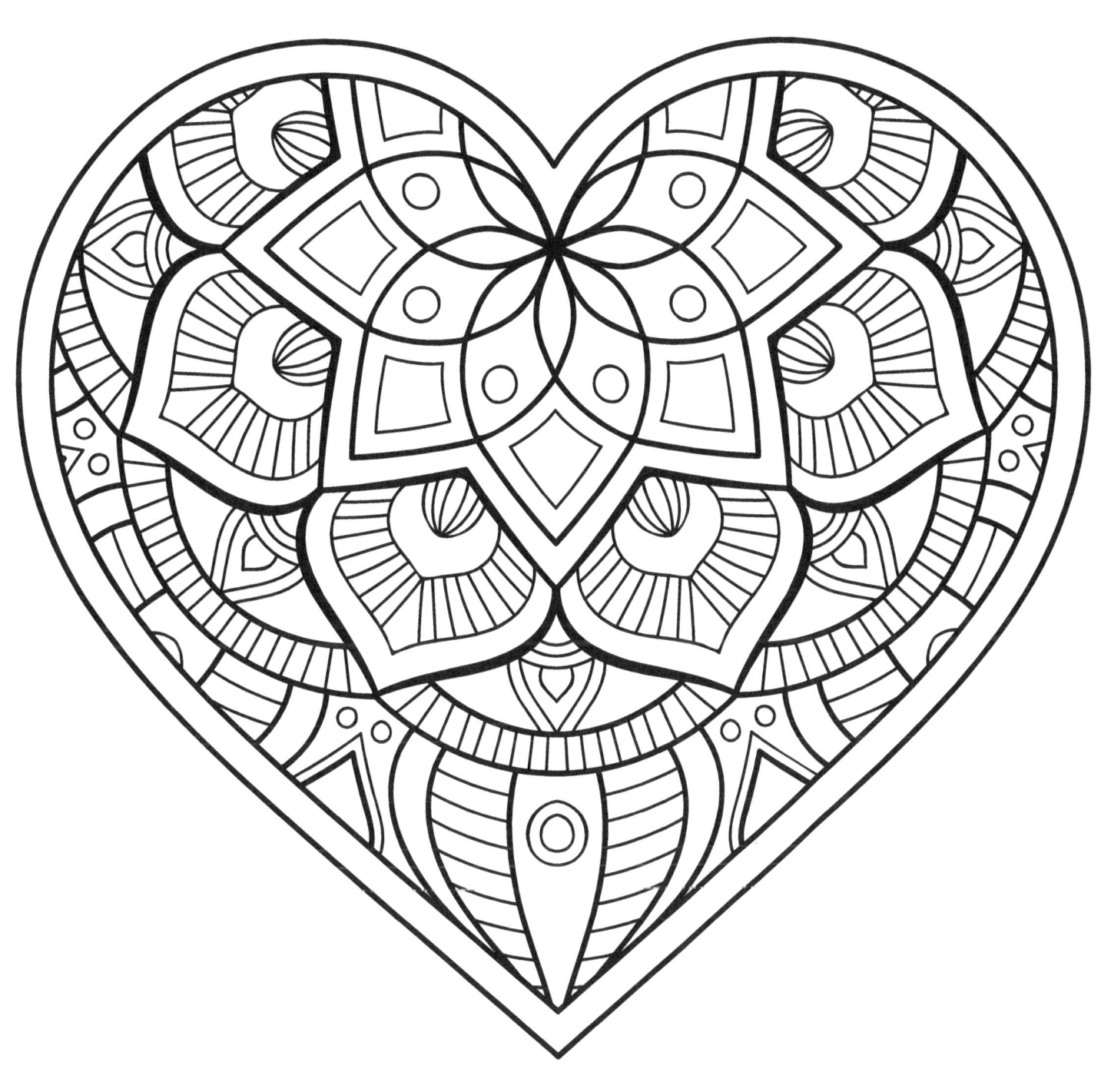

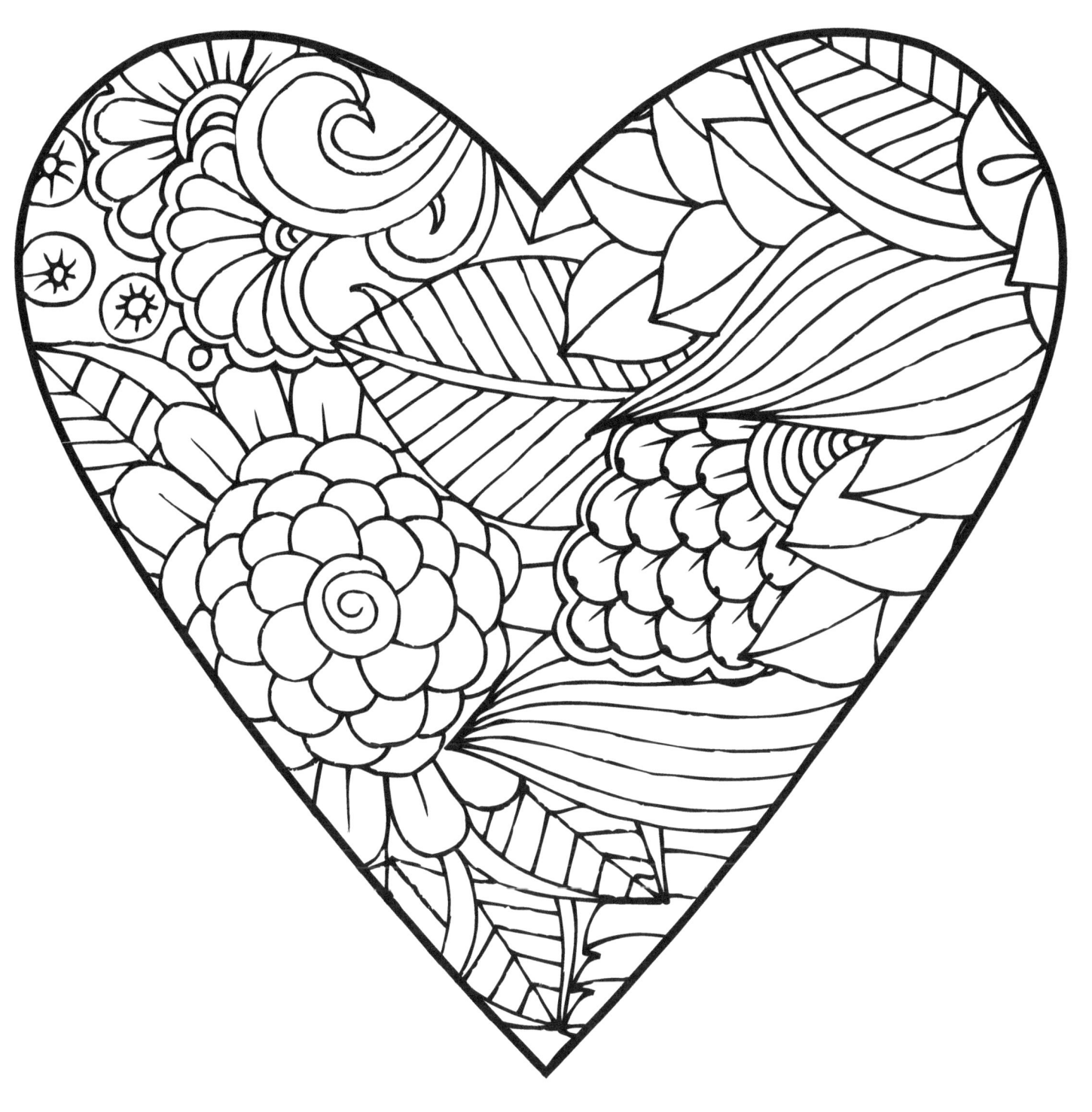

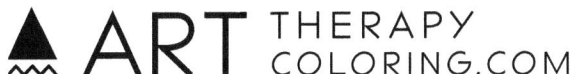

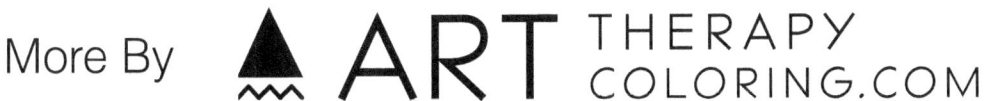

Best Selling Art Therapy Coloring Books

Coloring Books For Adults:

- Zombie Coloring Book: Black Background
- Butterfly Coloring Book For Adults: Black Background
- Tattoo Coloring Book: Black Background
- Coloring Books for Adults Relaxation: Native American Inspired Designs
- Fishing Coloring Book for Adults: Black Background

Coloring Books For Men:

- Coloring Book for Men: Anti-Stress Designs Vol 1
- Coloring Book For Men: Fishing Designs
- Coloring Book For Men: Tattoo Designs
- Coloring Books for Men: Hunting
- Coloring Book For Men: Biker Designs

Coloring Books For Seniors:

- Coloring Book For Seniors: Nature Designs Vol 1
- Coloring Book For Seniors: Anti-Stress Designs Vol 1
- Coloring Books for Seniors: Relaxing Designs
- Coloring Book For Seniors: Floral Designs Vol 1
- Coloring Book For Seniors: Ocean Designs Vol 1

Coloring Books For Teens and Tweens:

- Coloring Books For Teens: Ocean Designs
- Coloring Books for Teen Girls Vol 1
- Teen Inspirational Coloring Books
- Coloring Book for Teens: Anti-Stress Designs Vol 1
- Tween Coloring Books For Girls: Cute Animals

Coloring Books For Kids:

- Horse Coloring Book For Girls
- Coloring Books For Boys: Sharks
- Coloring Books for Boys: Animal Designs
- Unicorn Coloring Book for Girls
- Detailed Coloring Books For Kids

Coloring Books For Seniors

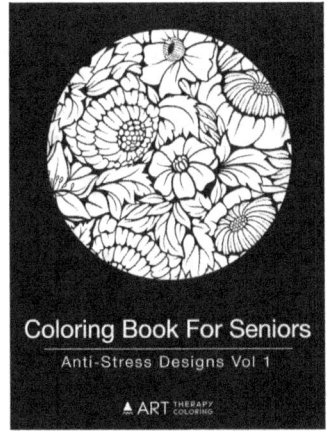

Coloring Book For Seniors
Anti-Stress Designs Vol 1

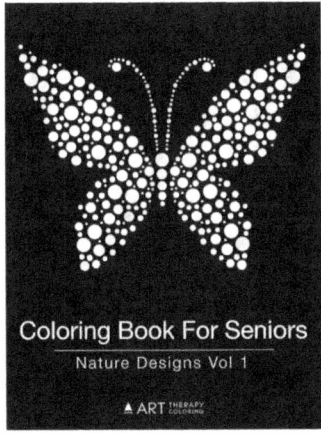

Coloring Book For Seniors
Nature Designs Vol 1

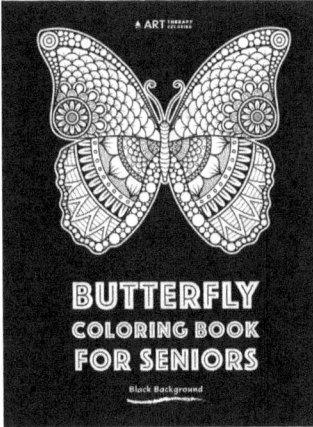

BUTTERFLY COLORING BOOK FOR SENIORS
Black Background

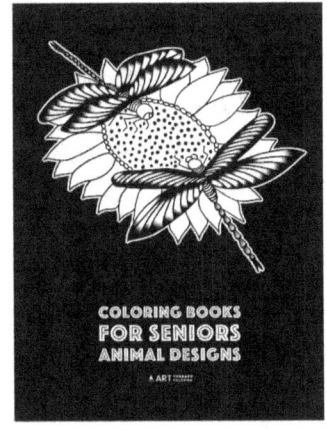

COLORING BOOKS FOR SENIORS ANIMAL DESIGNS

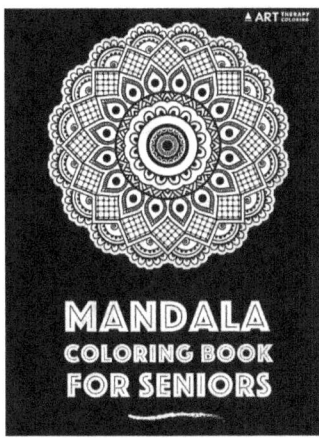

MANDALA COLORING BOOK FOR SENIORS

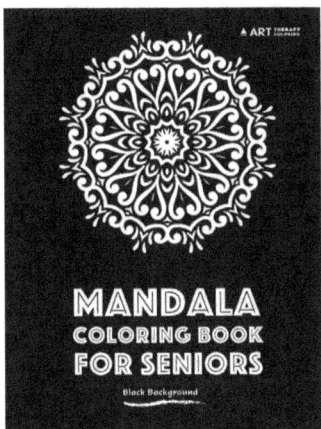

MANDALA COLORING BOOK FOR SENIORS
Black Background

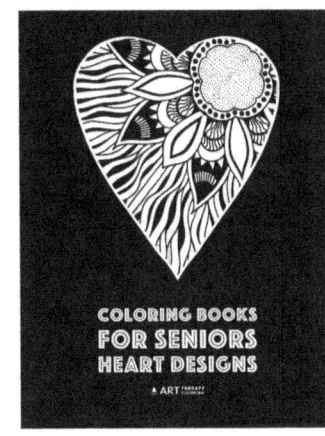

COLORING BOOKS FOR SENIORS HEART DESIGNS

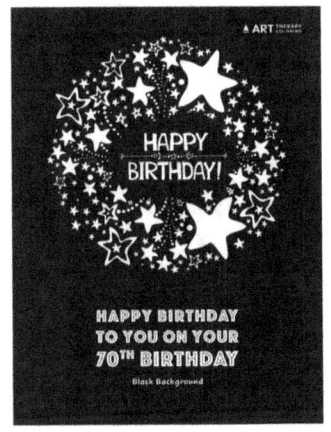

HAPPY BIRTHDAY TO YOU ON YOUR 70TH BIRTHDAY
Black Background

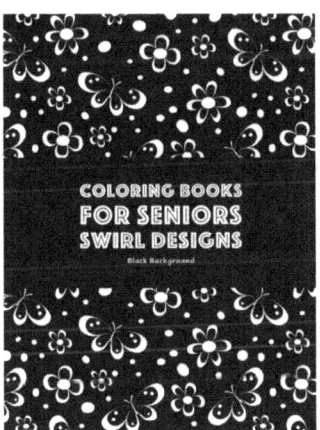

COLORING BOOKS FOR SENIORS SWIRL DESIGNS
Black Background

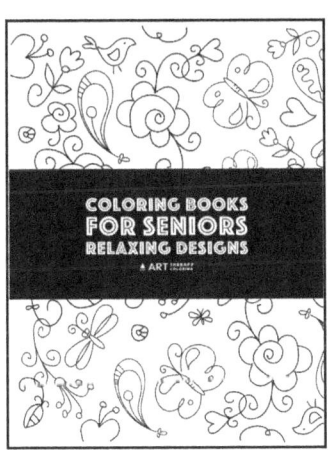

COLORING BOOKS FOR SENIORS RELAXING DESIGNS

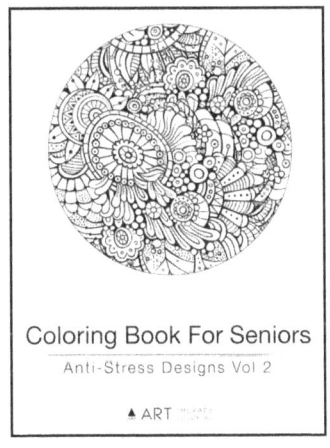

Coloring Book For Seniors
Anti-Stress Designs Vol 2

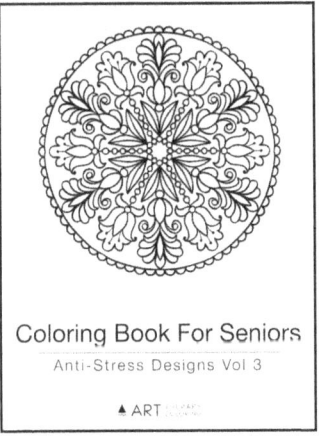

Coloring Book For Seniors
Anti-Stress Designs Vol 3

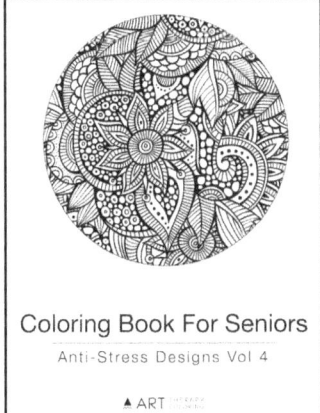

Coloring Book For Seniors
Anti-Stress Designs Vol 4

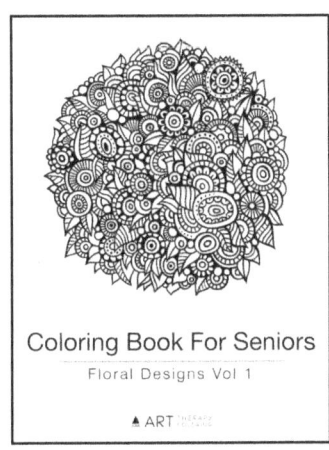

Coloring Book For Seniors
Floral Designs Vol 1

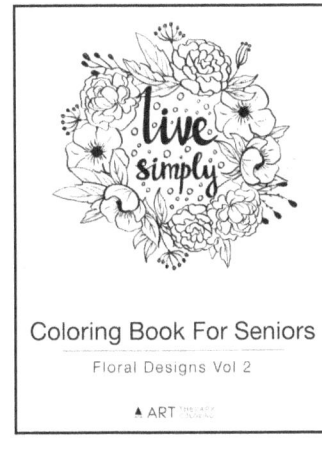

Coloring Book For Seniors
Floral Designs Vol 2

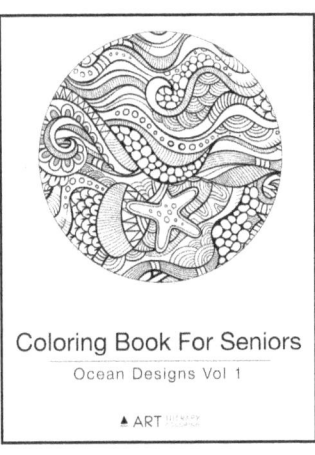

Coloring Book For Seniors
Ocean Designs Vol 1

Art Therapy Coloring Books

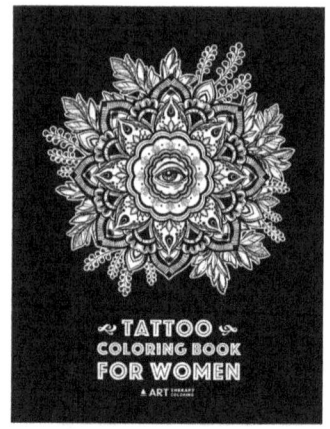

TATTOO
COLORING BOOK
FOR WOMEN

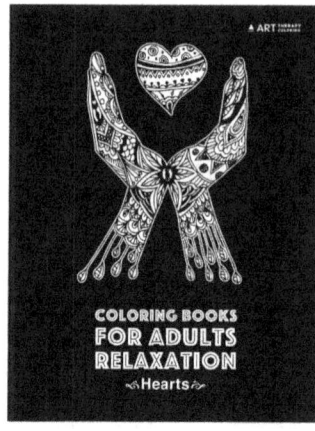

COLORING BOOKS
FOR ADULTS
RELAXATION
Hearts

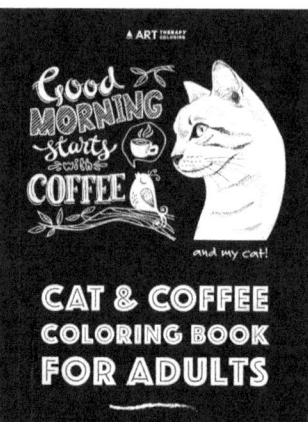

Good MORNING Starts with COFFEE
and my cat!

CAT & COFFEE
COLORING BOOK
FOR ADULTS

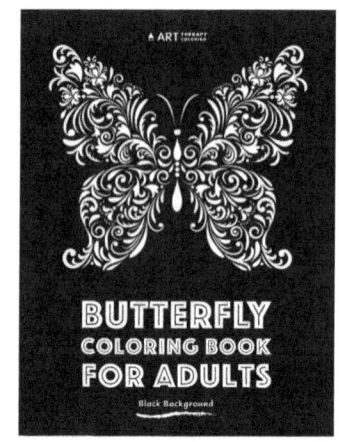

BUTTERFLY
COLORING BOOK
FOR ADULTS
Black Background

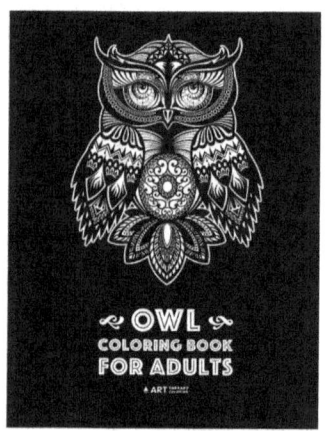

OWL
COLORING BOOK
FOR ADULTS

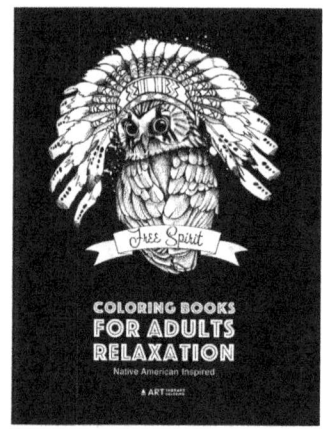

Free Spirit

COLORING BOOKS
FOR ADULTS
RELAXATION
Native American Inspired

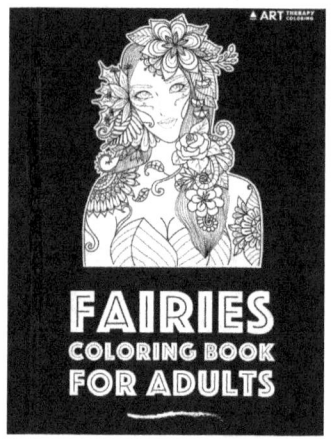

FAIRIES
COLORING BOOK
FOR ADULTS

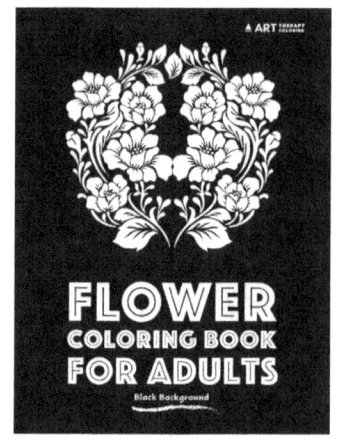

FLOWER
COLORING BOOK
FOR ADULTS
Black Background

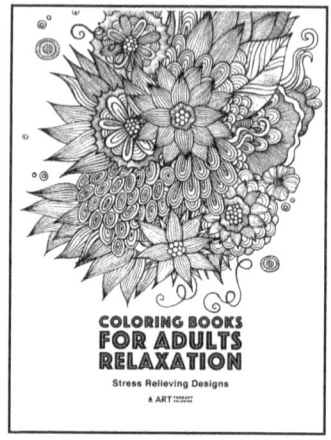

COLORING BOOKS
FOR ADULTS
RELAXATION
Stress Relieving Designs

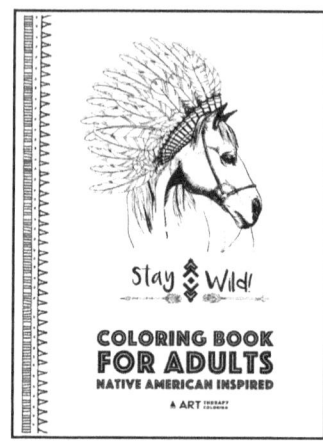

Stay Wild!

COLORING BOOK
FOR ADULTS
NATIVE AMERICAN INSPIRED

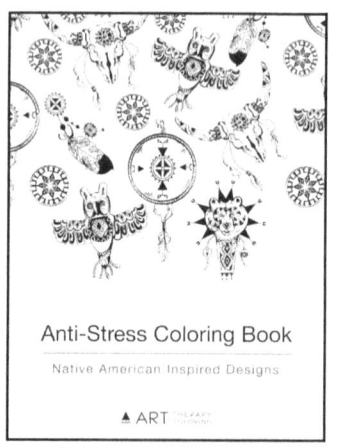

Anti-Stress Coloring Book
Native American Inspired Designs

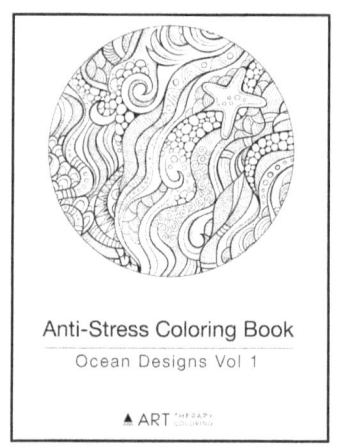

Anti-Stress Coloring Book
Ocean Designs Vol 1

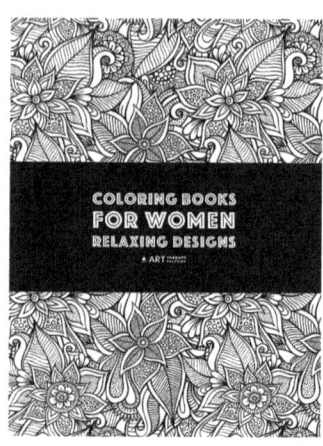

COLORING BOOKS
FOR WOMEN
RELAXING DESIGNS

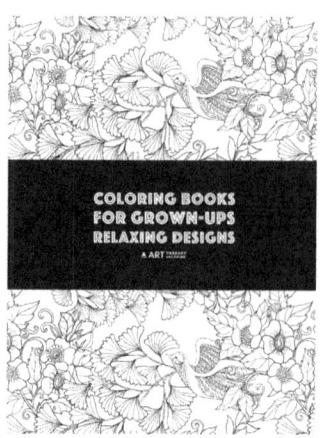

COLORING BOOKS
FOR GROWN-UPS
RELAXING DESIGNS

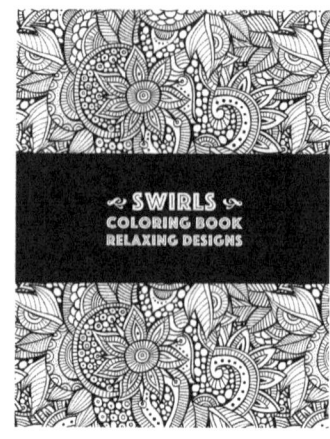

SWIRLS
COLORING BOOK
RELAXING DESIGNS

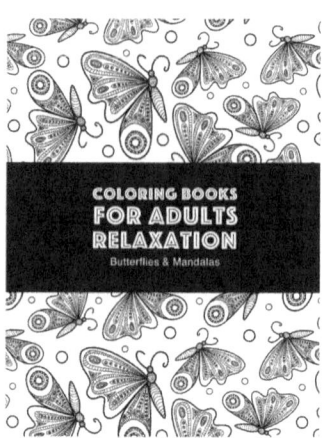

COLORING BOOKS
FOR ADULTS
RELAXATION
Butterflies & Mandalas

Art Therapy Coloring Books

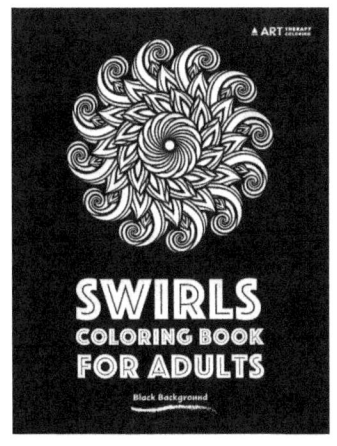

SWIRLS
COLORING BOOK
FOR ADULTS
Black Background

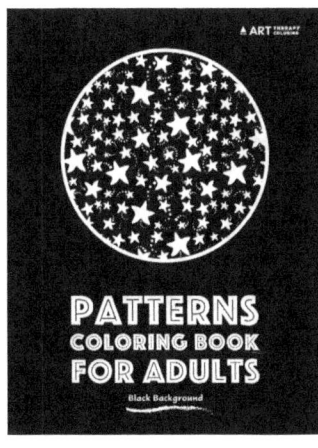

PATTERNS
COLORING BOOK
FOR ADULTS
Black Background

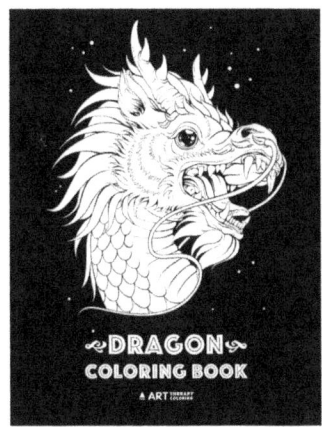

DRAGON
COLORING BOOK

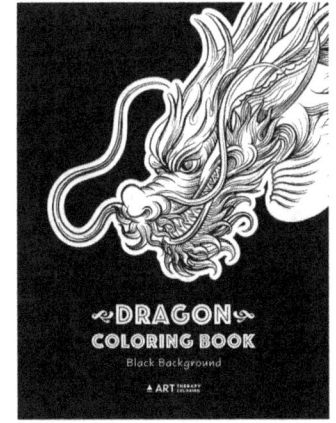

DRAGON
COLORING BOOK
Black Background

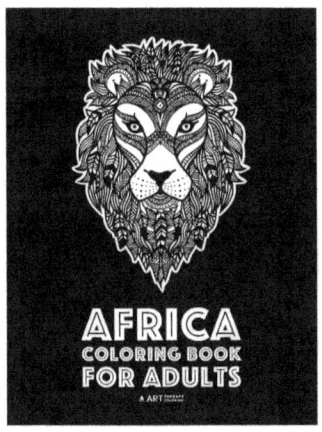

AFRICA
COLORING BOOK
FOR ADULTS

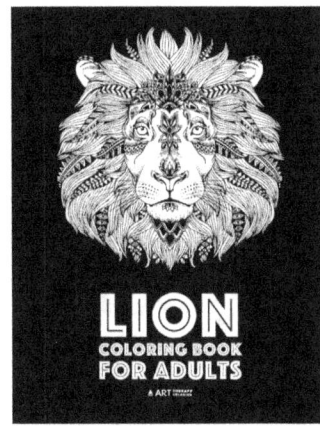

LION
COLORING BOOK
FOR ADULTS

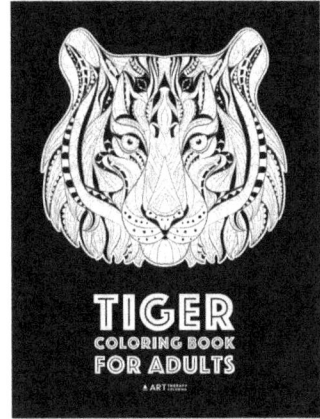

TIGER
COLORING BOOK
FOR ADULTS

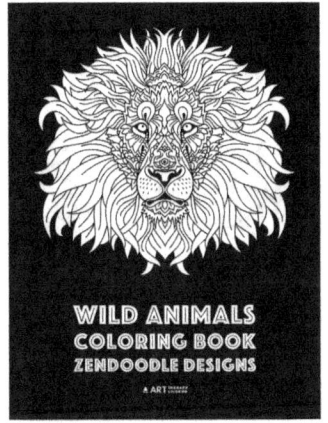

WILD ANIMALS
COLORING BOOK
ZENDOODLE DESIGNS

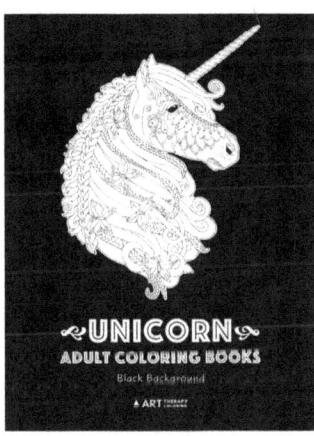

UNICORN
ADULT COLORING BOOKS
Black Background

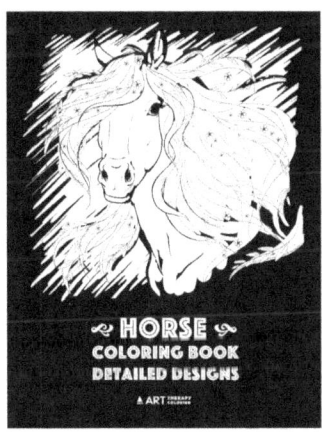

HORSE
COLORING BOOK
DETAILED DESIGNS

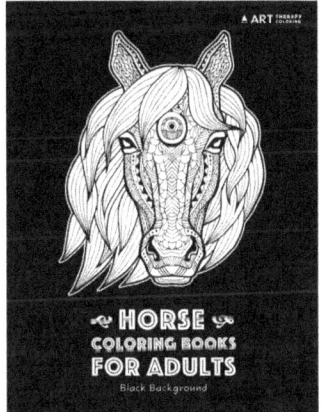

HORSE
COLORING BOOKS
FOR ADULTS
Black Background

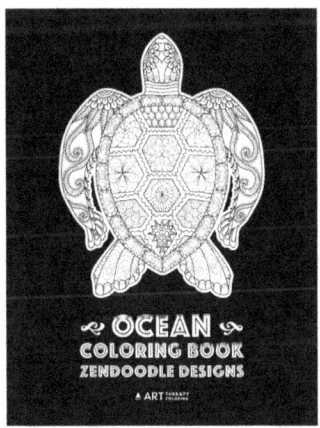

OCEAN
COLORING BOOK
ZENDOODLE DESIGNS

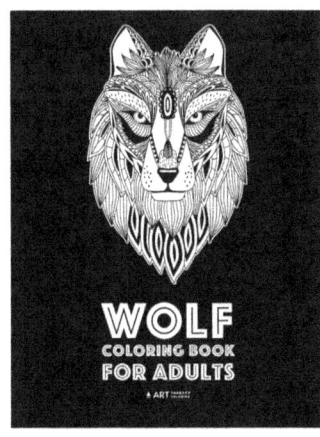

WOLF
COLORING BOOK
FOR ADULTS

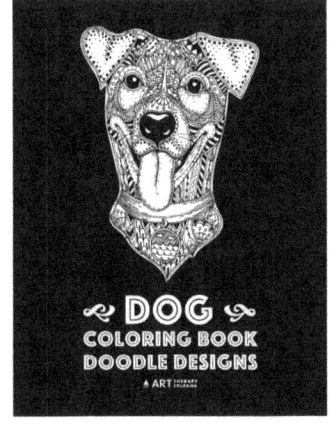

DOG
COLORING BOOK
DOODLE DESIGNS

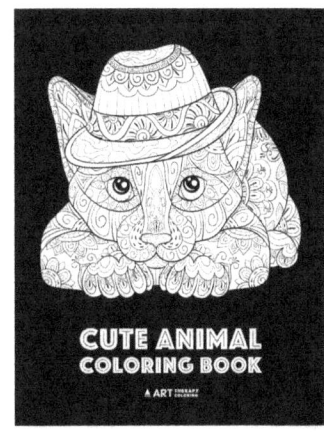

CUTE ANIMAL
COLORING BOOKS

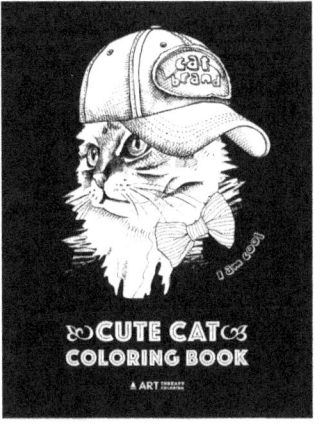

CUTE CAT
COLORING BOOK

Art Therapy Coloring Books

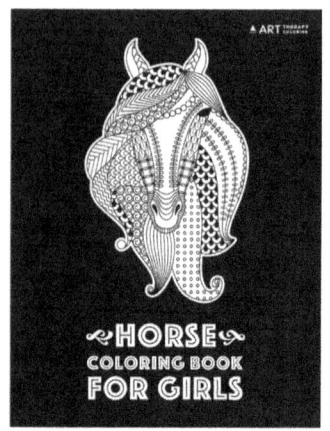

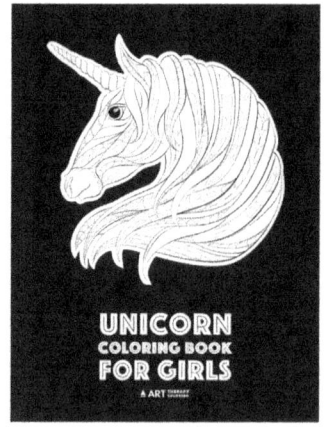

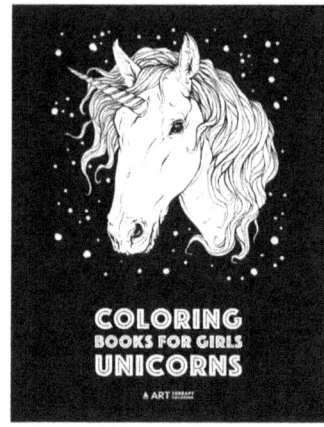

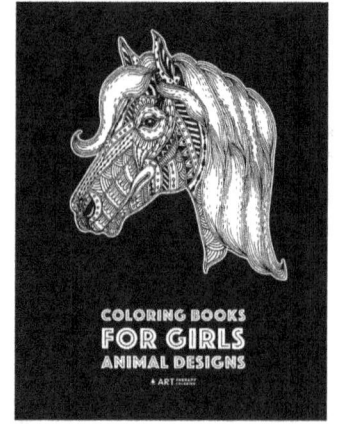

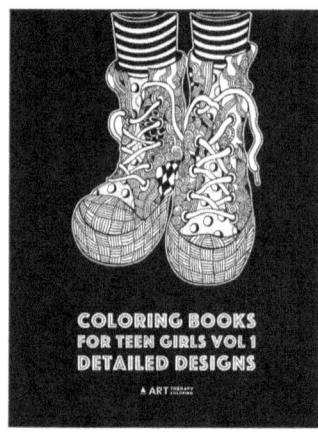

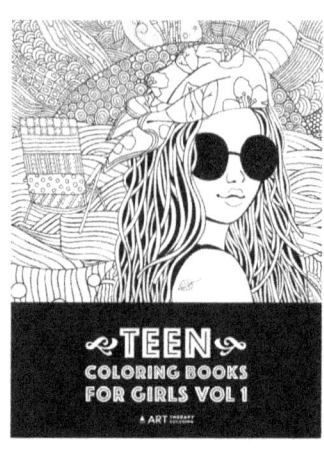

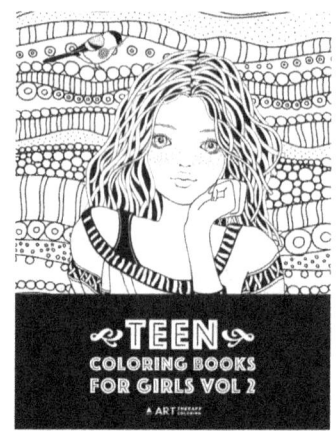

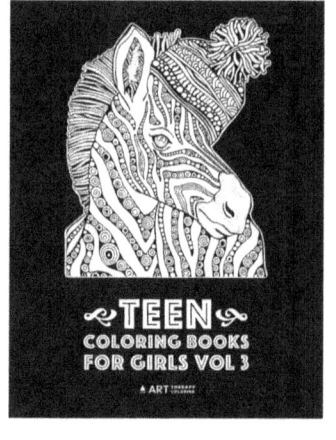

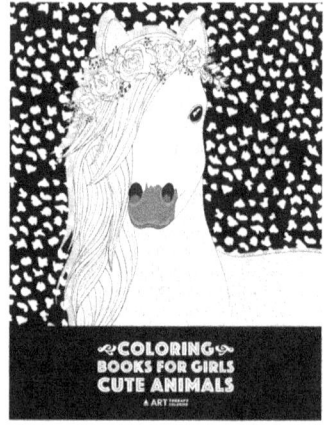

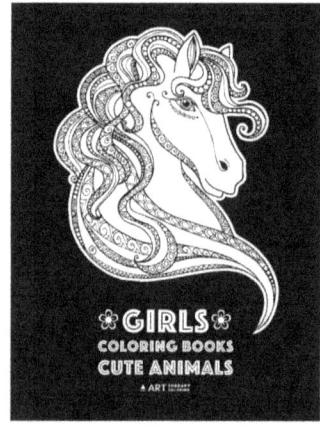

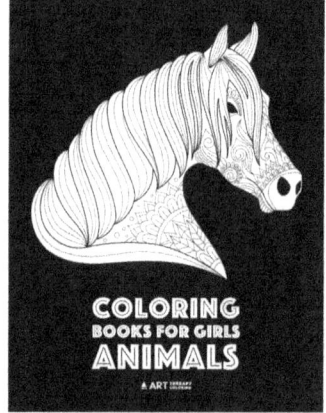

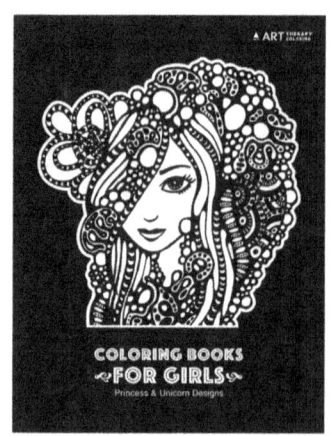

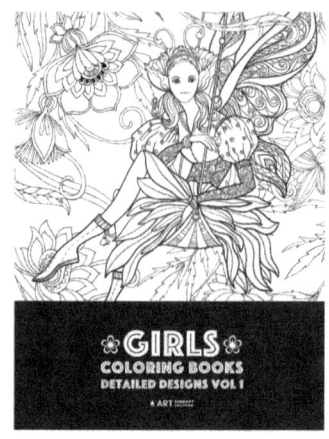

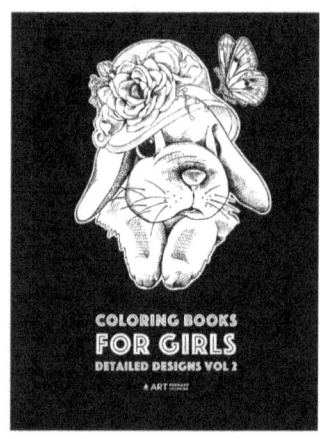

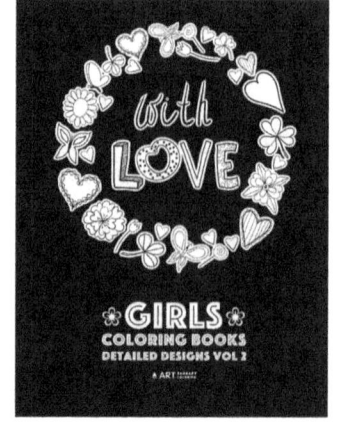

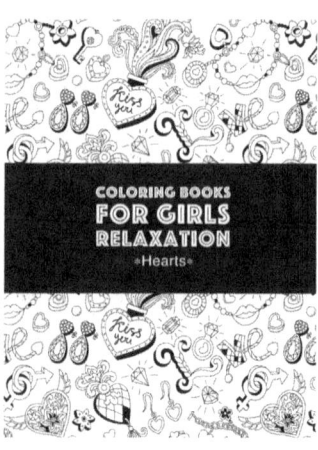

Art Therapy Coloring Books

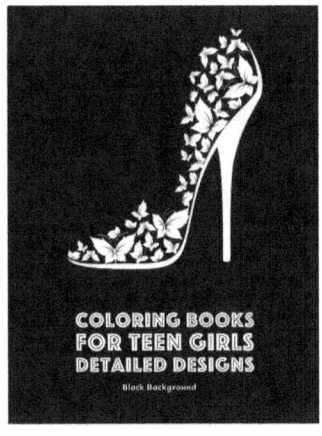

COLORING BOOKS FOR TEEN GIRLS DETAILED DESIGNS
Black Background

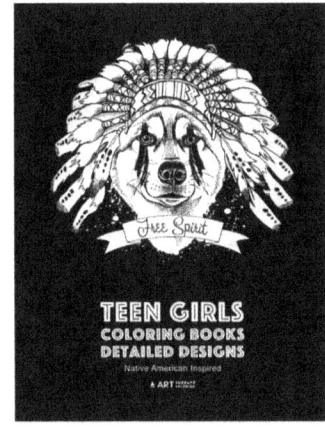

TEEN GIRLS COLORING BOOKS DETAILED DESIGNS
Native American Inspired

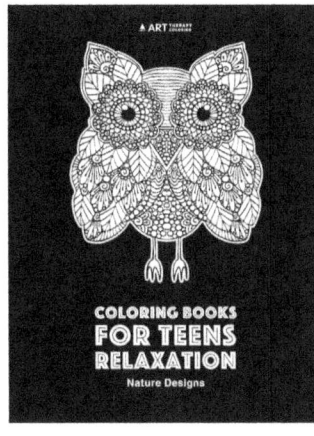

COLORING BOOKS FOR TEENS RELAXATION
Nature Designs

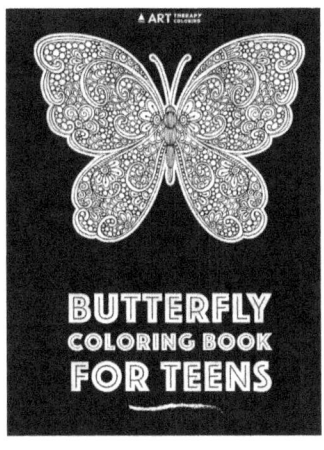

BUTTERFLY COLORING BOOK FOR TEENS

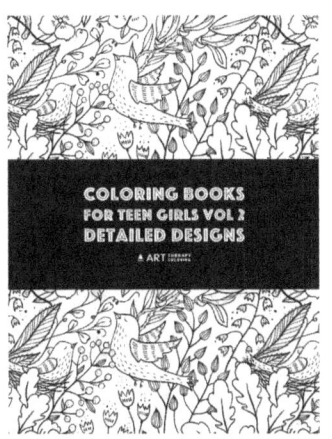

COLORING BOOKS FOR TEEN GIRLS VOL 2 DETAILED DESIGNS

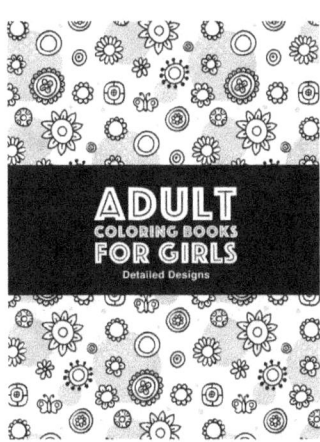

ADULT COLORING BOOKS FOR GIRLS
Detailed Designs

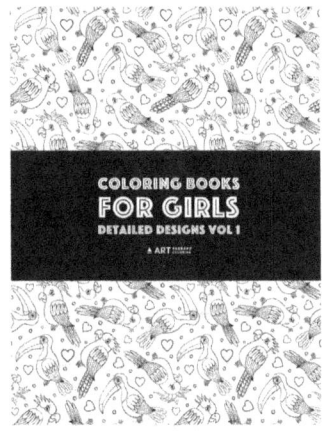

COLORING BOOKS FOR GIRLS DETAILED DESIGNS VOL 1

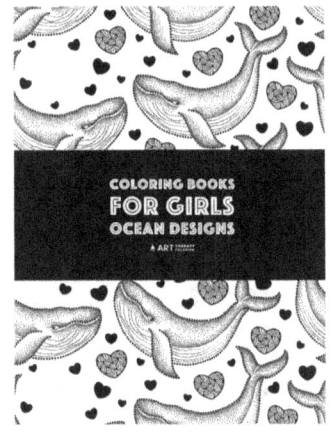

COLORING BOOKS FOR GIRLS OCEAN DESIGNS

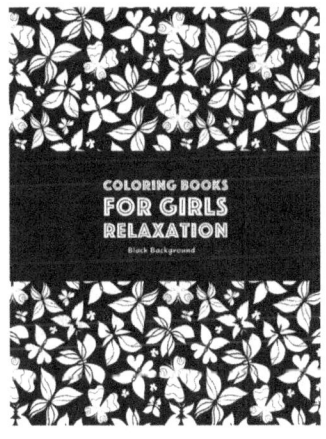

COLORING BOOKS FOR GIRLS RELAXATION
Black Background

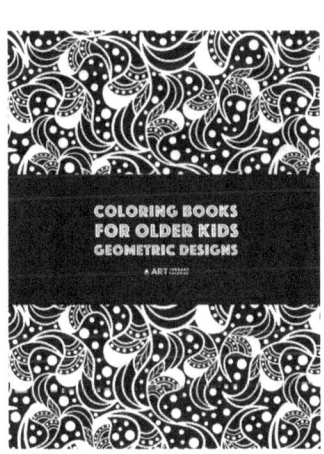

COLORING BOOKS FOR OLDER KIDS GEOMETRIC DESIGNS

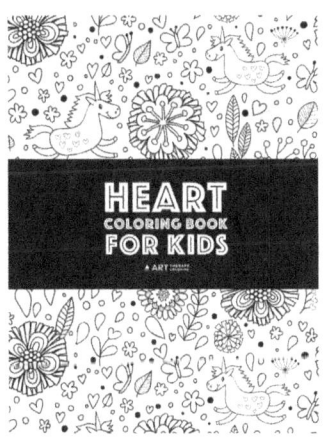

HEART COLORING BOOK FOR KIDS

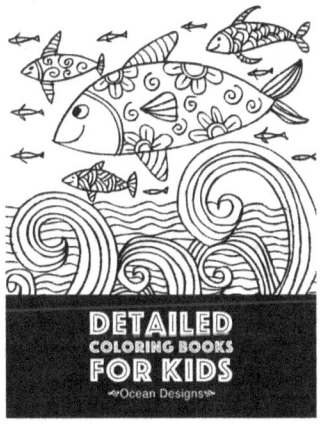

DETAILED COLORING BOOKS FOR KIDS
Ocean Designs

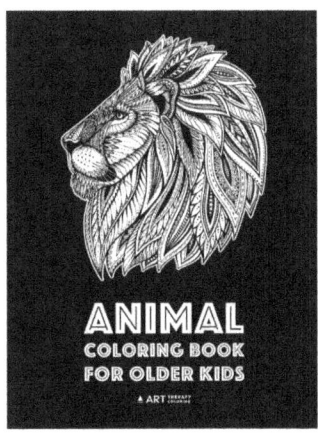

ANIMAL COLORING BOOK FOR OLDER KIDS

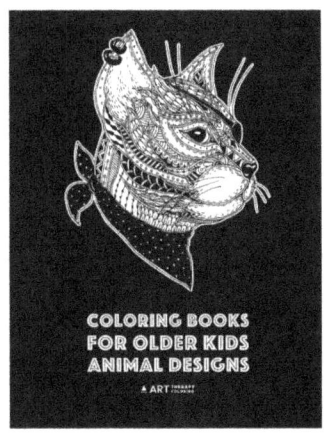

COLORING BOOKS FOR OLDER KIDS ANIMAL DESIGNS

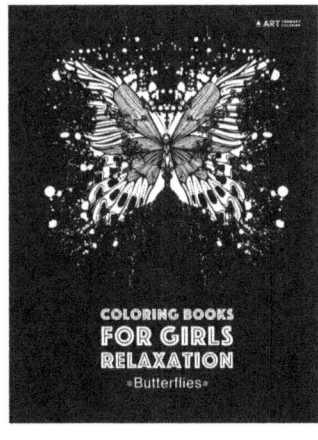

COLORING BOOKS FOR GIRLS RELAXATION
Butterflies

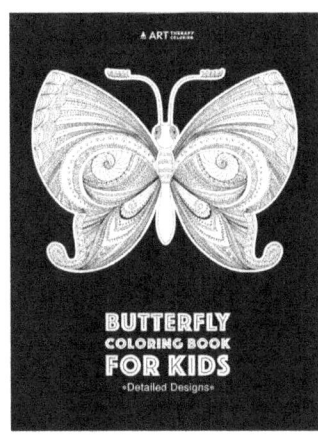

BUTTERFLY COLORING BOOK FOR KIDS
Detailed Designs

Art Therapy Coloring Books

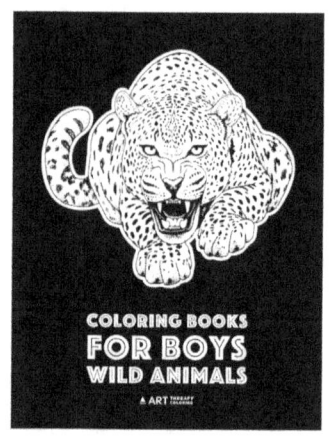

COLORING BOOKS FOR BOYS WILD ANIMALS

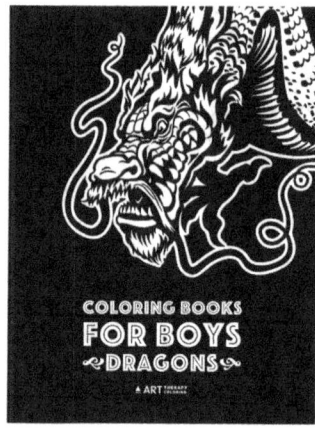

COLORING BOOKS FOR BOYS DRAGONS

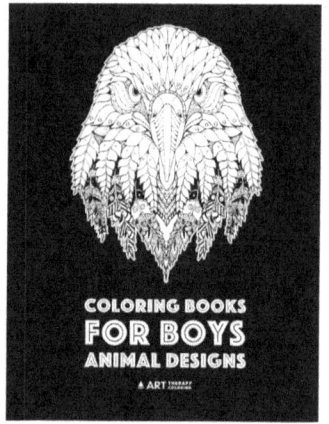

COLORING BOOKS FOR BOYS ANIMAL DESIGNS

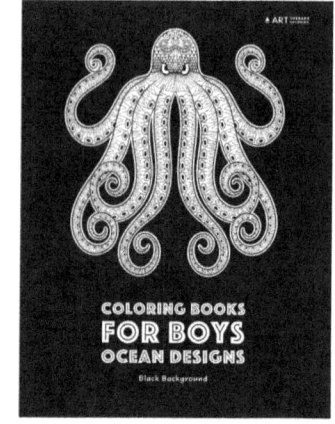

COLORING BOOKS FOR BOYS OCEAN DESIGNS
Black Background

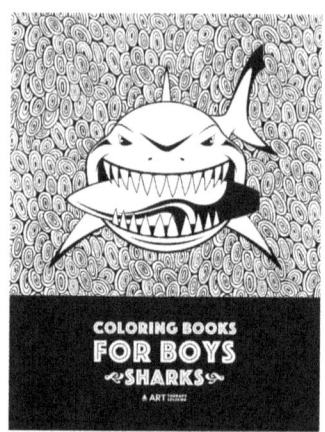

COLORING BOOKS FOR BOYS SHARKS

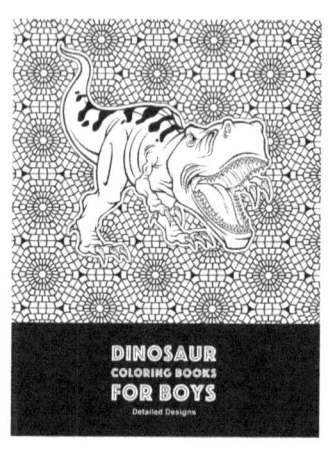

DINOSAUR COLORING BOOKS FOR BOYS
Detailed Designs

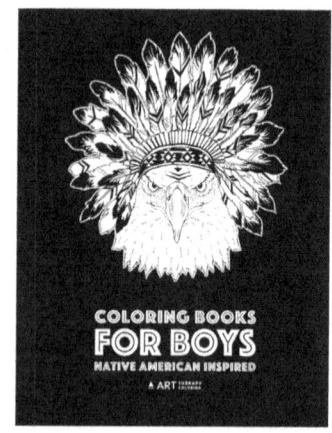

COLORING BOOKS FOR BOYS NATIVE AMERICAN INSPIRED

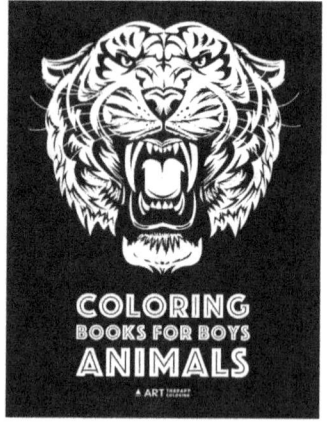

COLORING BOOKS FOR BOYS ANIMALS

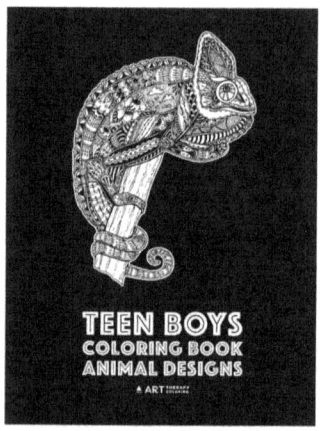

TEEN BOYS COLORING BOOK ANIMAL DESIGNS

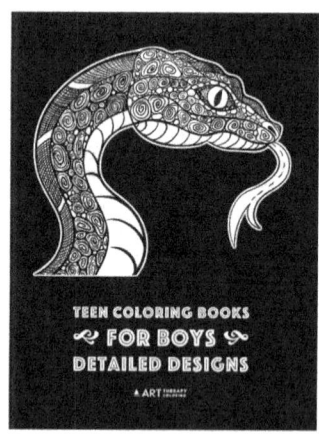

TEEN COLORING BOOKS FOR BOYS DETAILED DESIGNS

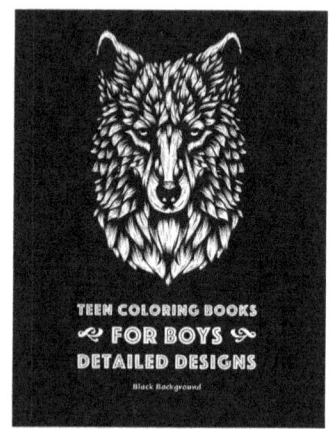

TEEN COLORING BOOKS FOR BOYS DETAILED DESIGNS
Black Background

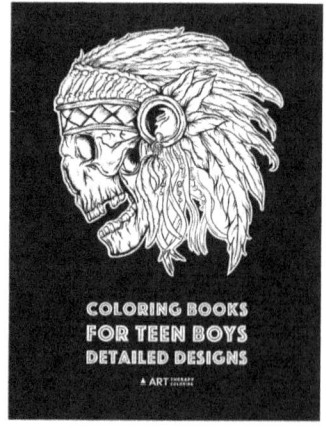

COLORING BOOKS FOR TEEN BOYS DETAILED DESIGNS

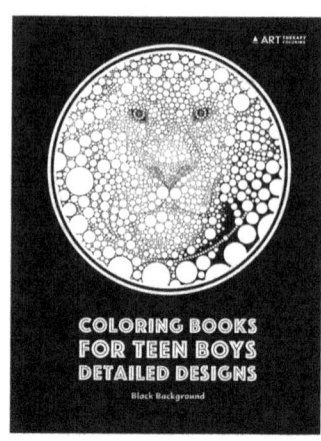

COLORING BOOKS FOR TEEN BOYS DETAILED DESIGNS
Black Background

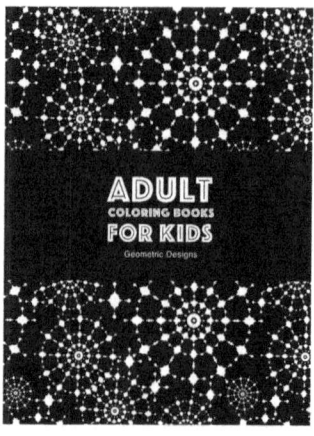

ADULT COLORING BOOKS FOR KIDS
Geometric Designs

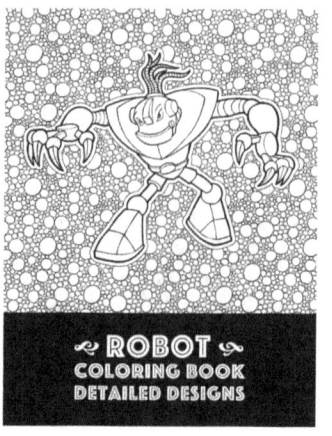

ROBOT COLORING BOOK DETAILED DESIGNS

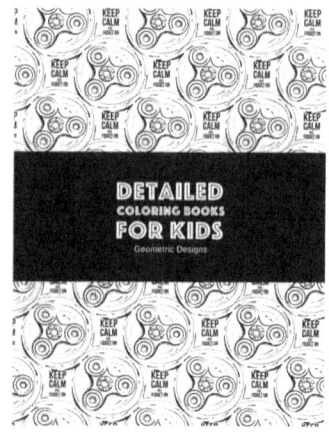

DETAILED COLORING BOOKS FOR KIDS
Geometric Designs

Art Therapy Coloring Books

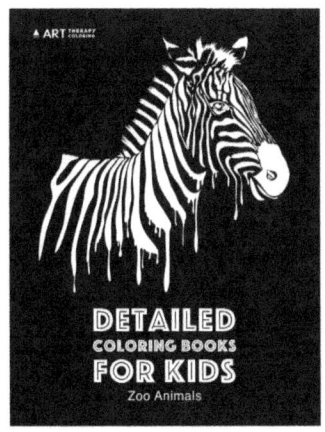

DETAILED
COLORING BOOKS
FOR KIDS
Zoo Animals

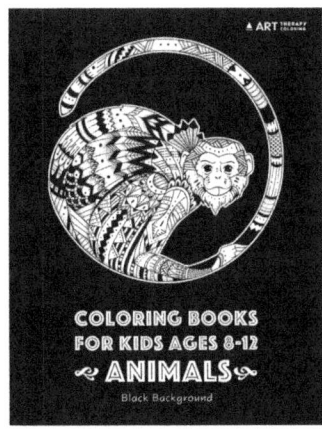

COLORING BOOKS
FOR KIDS AGES 8-12
ANIMALS
Black Background

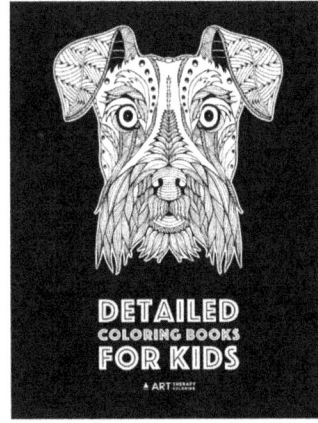

DETAILED
COLORING BOOKS
FOR KIDS

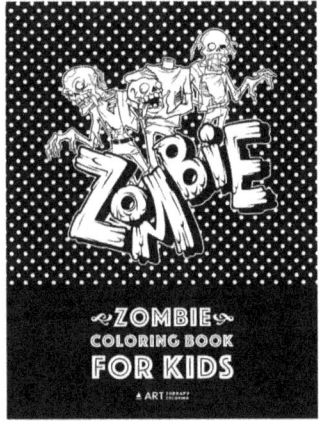

ZOMBIE
COLORING BOOK
FOR KIDS

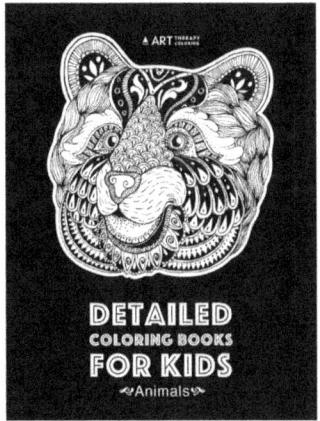

DETAILED
COLORING BOOKS
FOR KIDS
Animals

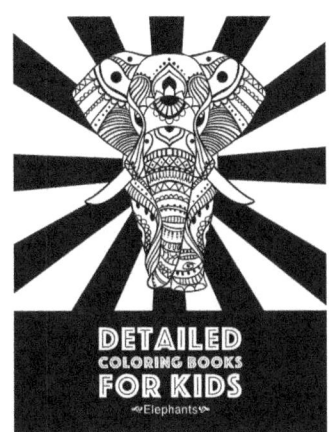

DETAILED
COLORING BOOKS
FOR KIDS
Elephants

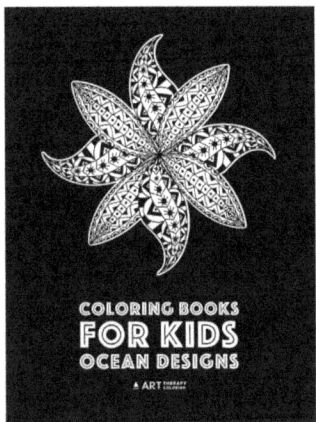

COLORING BOOKS
FOR KIDS
OCEAN DESIGNS

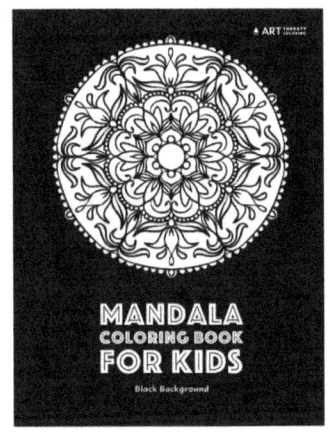

MANDALA
COLORING BOOK
FOR KIDS
Black Background

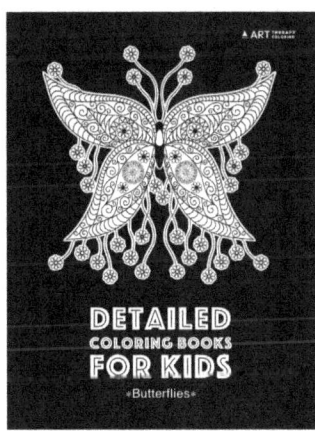

DETAILED
COLORING BOOKS
FOR KIDS
Butterflies

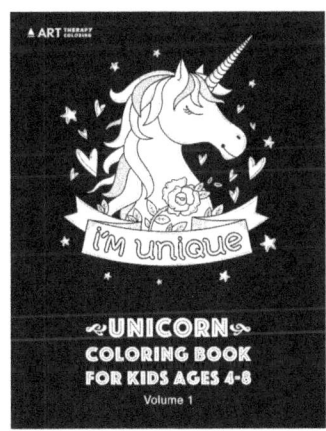

UNICORN
COLORING BOOK
FOR KIDS AGES 4-8
Volume 1

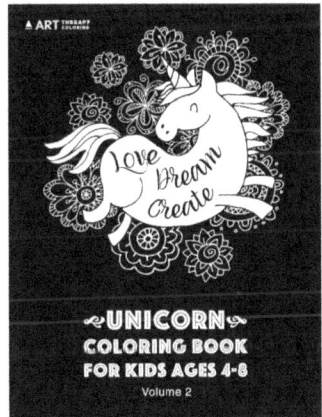

UNICORN
COLORING BOOK
FOR KIDS AGES 4-8
Volume 2

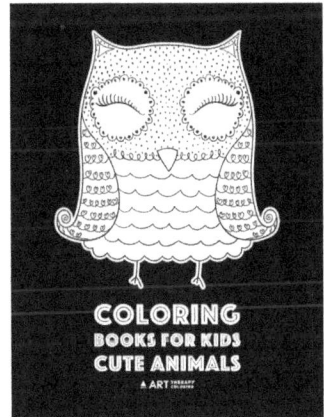

COLORING
BOOKS FOR KIDS
CUTE ANIMALS

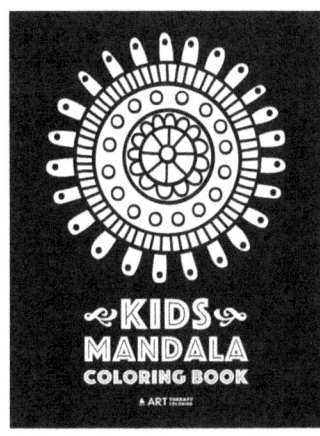

**KIDS
MANDALA**
COLORING BOOK

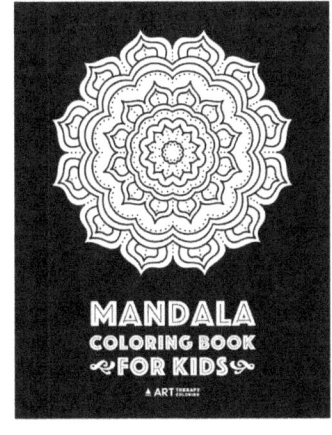

MANDALA
COLORING BOOK
FOR KIDS

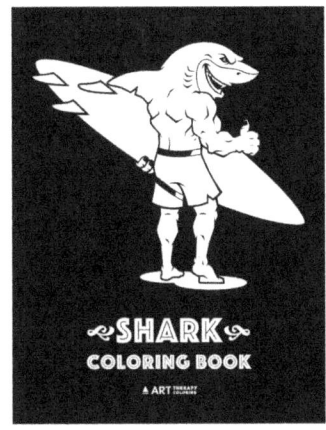

SHARK
COLORING BOOK

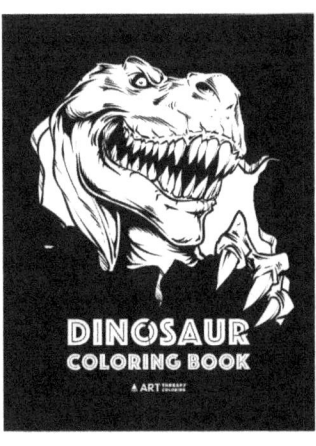

DINOSAUR
COLORING BOOK

Coloring Books For Seniors
Heart Designs

Published by:
Art Therapy Coloring
www.arttherapycoloring.com

Shutterstock Images

ISBN: 978-1-64126-070-1